# Starr Gazing

*Stories of Buffalo,*

*the Niagara Region, and Beyond*

..............................................

Daniel P. Starr

Buffalo, NY

2018

For more information contact:

Joseph F. Bieron, Publisher

Canisius College

2001 Main Street

Buffalo, NY 14208

Book and Cover Design: Rebecca Francisco

ISBN 978-0-9885895-6-8

Printed in the United States of America

# Table of Contents

# Foreword

It has been my good fortune to know Dan Starr for over fifty years as colleagues and friends on the faculty at Canisius College. In a way, we experienced similar academic careers, following divergent pathways along the way; Dan began his career in the History Department at the college and taught American History for many years. He then made a significant career change and became Director of Athletics at the college. He served for over 25 years and to characterize his service as memorable and successful is an understatement. He was elected to the college's Sports Hall of Fame as well as to the Buffalo Sports Hall of Fame.

I taught Chemistry for 35 years, and was Dean of Arts and Sciences for eight years, but along the way, I pursued my love of history and founded Canisius College Press that published books on topics of local history.

Our interests and close friendship resulted in a book that Starr authored and Bieron published in 2009 entitled, "The Golden Age of Buffalo Sports 1945-1950." Dan continued his writing by authoring a semi-monthly column of Buffalo stories in a local community newspaper, "After Fifty", a publication aimed at a readership of senior citizens.

This background information explains the origin to a proposal for a book, modeled after a very successful book published by Bieron in the early days of the Canisius College Press. George Kunz, as a freelance writer, had written short stories for the Buffalo Evening News. After his death, his family asked CC Press to publish a collection of his stories. "Buffalo Memories" was the book published and it has sold over 15,000 copies and can still be found in local bookstores.

Based on our experiences in promoting local history by writing and publishing books, we proposed a book that would be a collection of Dan's articles written over a period of nine years. "Starr Gazing" is the product of our efforts.

The book is eclectic in form. When you search for this term in the dictionary, the definitions are "selecting what appears to be best in various venues… composed of elements drawn from various sources." This is a good description of the book.

Each chapter, composed of articles of similar content, originate from experiences in Dan's life, many from the 1940s and 1950s, basketball in the Aud, sports well known in Buffalo lore, outdoor amusements like Crystal Beach, well-known taverns, popular teenage activities from yesteryear, breakfast gatherings of senior friends and memorable landmarks from a once great city.

If you are a teenager, you probably will not relate to this book, so it will not be featured on YouTube or published as an e-book. However, the book should appeal to any senior citizen, especially those who were born and raised in Western New York. Old timers will recall their own experiences, sometimes in more detail, in venues that Dan describes.

This is a book written for senior citizens, with each story only a few pages long. It is perfect bedtime reading, one or two stories and you fall asleep. The next day, you can pick up the book, read a new story and have pleasant memories about a very different experience.

Joseph F. Bieron
June 2018

# Acknowledgements

Writing has been an important part of my retirement years. Retirement, in general, has suited me just fine. I exercise regularly. I spend time with family, especially with grandchildren in their early years. I enjoy breakfasts and lunches with many friends, and I do a variety of volunteer work. And I enjoy writing.

Some years ago, I met the editor/publisher of After 50, Phyllis Gorski and Bonnie DeGweck. They offered me the opportunity to write a monthly column for After 50, a community newspaper aimed at seniors. Now, about 100 columns later, things have worked out fine. I have the freedom to write about almost anything that comes to mind. I am sure that they knew a retiree of my vintage was not about to fill their newspaper with salacious material or Bolshevik propaganda.

My main contact with after 50 News is Amy DeGweck-Hallborg. Amy runs the office. She would be properly regarded as the Point Person. She has been of tremendous assistance to me; offering advice and suggestions, and in finding appropriate photos. It is a pleasure working with Amy.

As for this book, this collection of columns, Dr. Joseph Bieron is the responsible citizen who took the initiative. Joe Bieron has been a trusted colleague for over half a century and a very good friend to boot. Joe has had some valuable experience publishing and editing books and he thought it might be worthwhile to assemble a numbers of my columns and publish them as a book. I am very grateful to Joe.

My thanks also go to my daughter Kate. Kate had done considerable editing for the US State Department in Washington. She reads my monthly effort, makes the necessary corrections in addition to offering suggestions. Another daughter, Jennifer, also with writing experience, has helped to make my columns more readable.

My thanks also to Rhianna Miller. Rhianna is more or less Joe Bieron's administrative assistant. When not flying in a private plane over the Adirondack Mountains, Rhianna was busy playing a major role in organizing and preparing the materials for the book.

# Preface

There was no common theme to my columns although I would say that many of them were about the period of my youth (often that is the most memorable period of peoples' lives). I refer to the 1940-50s, the World War II era. Since part of my working life involved college athletics, several columns do pertain to sports. Many columns focus on a variety of developments in Buffalo and Western New York in general.

In other words, the contents of the book are eclectic. I also took the liberty of often including the names of personal friends and acquaintances. Occasionally I have written about a milestone, a 100th anniversary or even a 50th.

# Chapter 1. The City of Buffalo

*Buffalo, early in the 20th century was a top ten city. The downtown Statler Hotel was a fitting symbol of the Queen City's status. Buffalo has successfully "downsized" since then, but its ethnic populations continue to play an important role.*

## Buffalo: Mid-Size and Liking It
Originally printed June 2013

*A century ago, actually at the time of Buffalo's hosting the Pan American Exhibition, Buffalo was a top ten city in the U.S. Today, after experiencing some up and down times in the past century, Buffalo has been "reborn" and has emerged as an attractive mid-size city.*

Finally, we (Buffalonians/Western New Yorkers – used interchangeably) are accepting the inevitable and coping with it nicely. I refer to the fact that Buffalo is no longer the major city it was a century ago. We are now a mid-size city.

In 1900, Buffalo was ranked 8th in population in the US; as late as 1940/50 we were in the top 15, ahead of Atlanta and Dallas. Presently Buffalo is #72. Our metropolitan area is 49th. *14-73 (when I was growing up.)*

### Buffalo: in the 1940s/50's
The "After 50 (or 75) set": nostalgically recalls Buffalo harbor, one of the busiest inland ports in the US. Freighters moved by tugboats constantly jockeying for dock space. WNY was an industrial giant. If you drove along the Niagara River from Buffalo to Niagara Falls, you encountered an incredible variety

of heavy industry: General Motors, Dunlop, DuPont, numerous oil refineries, Western Electric, Durez, Hooker Chemical, Union Carbide, Carborundum and more. Steel mills in Lackawanna and South Buffalo were huge. That was just a fraction of the area's industrial might.

A thriving downtown was home to prosperous department stores such as JN Adam and Hengerer's, and top of the line retailers including Kleinhans, Flint and Kent, and Berger's. Nearby were major theaters, restaurants, hotels, jazz bars, nightclubs, and smack in the middle of Shelton Square, stood the Palace Burlesk. Main Street appeared to be a smaller version of the NYC's Great White Way. Memorial Auditorium was part of the scene, used for many events, in addition to hockey and basketball. Civic Stadium (not just for football), and the historic Offermann Baseball Park were not far away.

In the 40's and 50's, when young people were looking for something to do, they headed downtown; when mothers wanted to shop, they went downtown; when couples wanted to "go out" they went downtown. Downtown Buffalo was the vital center of action, but it would not last.

### In-between years, 1960's – 90's: Industrial Giant to Rustbelt symbol

Industries moved south and west; workers followed. The rustbelt set in. Retailers rushed to the suburbs. Downtown Buffalo became a ghost town. The city was referred to as "the armpit of the East." Visitors from our sister city, Dortmund, Germany, in the 1980's could not believe the emptiness that engulfed downtown. True, sports teams still drew big numbers. Fans flocked to the "Rockpile" in the 60's to watch the NFL Bills. As soon as the final whistle blew, those fans headed back to the suburbs. The same happened with the Sabres in Memorial Auditorium. Mayor Jimmy Griffin built a new baseball stadium, but again the nearby eating and drinking establishments went dry, thirsting for new business. Who in their right mind wanted to "hang out" in Buffalo? Sportswriter Phil Ranallo ended one of his classic columns with: "Will the last one out (of Buffalo) please turn off the lights?"

But positive changes were afoot; momentum accelerated by the turn of this century.

### A mid-size Buffalo – alive and well in the 21st century.

A new century dawns; there is a lot going on. Recently we have heard much about the rejuvenated Harbor/Canal area and the sprawling Buffalo/Niagara Medical Complex.

Four areas (architecture, food, the medical complex, and harbor place), do much to enhance Buffalo's reputation. So do the Bills and Sabres – though it would help if they won more often.

No need to elaborate here; others have already done so.

But it is worth noting other things that make our area such a wonderful place to live and a terrific place to visit; one of the very best in the entire country.

Weather is one. Yes, weather! Hey, if you are looking for natural disasters, don't come here. For tornadoes visit the South and the Plains; for droughts Texas and the Southwest; floods, the Midwest; mudslides, earthquakes visit California; for hurricanes, check the entire Atlantic Coast. For weird snowfalls in September or April, try self-inflated Denver. For clammy, soggy weather – it's the Northwest. Okay, South Florida is exceptionally nice.

Yes, we get snow and the media will not let us forget the Blizzard of '77. I readily admit that by the time March rolls around in Buffalo, I long for some milder weather. Still we do not have the long, harsh Minnesota winters. Overall we have wonderful weather, warm summers, pleasant springs, colorful autumns, and some pretty good winters - with most of the snow falling south for the benefit of the ski fanatics.

There is more. We have a new efficient airport terminal – easy to access. We have a splendid parks system (thanks to Olmsted), and magnificent cultural institutions. To name just a few, Buffalo is home to the crème de la crème Buffalo Philharmonic, impressive art galleries, the Allentown Art Festival, Shakespeare in the Park and a very popular zoo. We also have a pretty good daily newspaper, The Buffalo News, and access to excellent radio stations, both local and Canadian. True- the 2nd Peace Bridge may not be resolved in the present century. Not much retailing will return to downtown. We do need more public beaches.

We do NOT have perpetual traffic congestion (though you might have to wait for two light changes at Parkside and the Scajaquada).

There is more. Canada is a stone's throw away. When I served as Athletics Director at Canisius, I used to tell the parents of recruits: "If you get a little tired of Buffalo, just 90 miles away is a world class city, Toronto has something for everyone" (that's another column?).

The Buffalo/Western New York that we see in this 2nd decade of the 21st century is progressing quite well.

*Buffalo's Busy Harbor 1940 – Before the Skyway was built*

*Main St 1930s - Downtown Buffalo - showing Century Theater, Hengerers Dept. store*

*Two Buffalo Celebrities, music historian, Chuck Mancuso and legendary pianist, Jackie Jacko*

## Buffalo's Statler Hotel – A 20th Century Monument
Originally printed March 2010

*For most of the 20th century, the Statler was THE hotel in downtown Buffalo. Today, with harbor place and canal side setting the pace for rejuvenated downtown Buffalo, many grand new hotels have been built. But for many years, the 18 story Statler was in a class by itself.*

When "After 50" types think of spectacular big city hotels, invariably at the top of the list would be the Waldorf in NYC, the Royal York in Toronto, the Mayflower in D.C., and, of course, the Statler in Buffalo.

Flagship of the Statler chain, Buffalo's grandest hotel opened in the "roaring 20's;" fittingly an era when Buffalo was rated among the major cities in the U.S. In the top 15 in population, Buffalo was thriving in industry, commerce, and entertainment.

The soaring hotel symbolized the city. Standing astride Niagara Square, it eventually overlooked several government buildings, city, county, state and federal, as well as the monument to President William McKinley. Nearby was the Erlanger Theater, which featured the best of Broadway. A short distance away were the theaters, restaurants, department stores and office buildings that kept the city busy night and day.

It was the interior of the Statler that was truly striking. To the immediate left of the main entrance and down a few steps was the Rendezvous Room.

There the Max Miller Band featuring Ray Mauszewski often performed. Up a few stairs was the imposing main lobby with its high ceilings, marble construction, attractive velvet tapestries and serenely placed potted plants.

To the left was the Golden Ballroom, where hundreds of guests wined, dined and danced under crystal chandeliers, golden trimmings and other richly embellished appointments. Dining invariably ended with waiters parading trays of flaming Baked Alaska; dancing was often to the music of Harold Austin or Irv Shire but sometimes to the big bands of Vaughn Monroe, Carmen Cavallaro or Frankie Carle.

To the right of the lobby was the beautiful Terrace Room where dining was elegant and the Sunday brunch a tradition. The high graceful windows afforded excellent views of Niagara Square.

Straight ahead were the registration desk, elevators, brass fixtures, and neatly dressed bellhops, closely resembling the "Call for Johnny" Philip Morris character. Further along was the bar, the scene of lively nighttime activity. The locals referred to it as the Statler Bar, as in "Meet you after work at the Statler Bar." Tony Carnevale at the piano provided the atmosphere.

On the mezzanine were offices, flower and gift shops and a popular beauty salon; in the basement were a multi chaired barbershop, a Turkish bath and a swimming pool. Also on the first level were coffee shops, restaurants, airline ticket outlets, and banking and insurance offices. The second level housed the Chamber of Commerce as well as several function rooms, used for business meetings, conferences and cocktail parties. The Frontier Press Club as well as the Rotary, the Zonta and other service clubs met regularly. The upper floors had hundreds of guest rooms. On the 18th floor was the number one radio station WBEN, home of Buffalo morning icon, Clint Buehlmann, "yours truly Buelly."

Almost every Buffalo native has special memories of the Statler. The Golden Ballroom itself was the scene of one of the most memorable. In 1930 at a Canisius football banquet, Knute Rockne, the greatest college football coach ever, gave one of his last speeches; a short time later he died in a plane crash.

In 1945, a St. Joe's – Canisius High School sports banquet featured Jim Thorpe, the greatest athlete of the era, as main speaker. A few days after the event, Thorpe's host received a call from the Statler manager saying that Thorpe was still in his room and had run up a pretty hefty room service tab. Thorpe left shortly thereafter.

At an NCAA convention some years ago, I chatted with a friend, Chuck Neinas, Commissioner of the College Football Association. He mentioned his participation in the Canisius sponsored Queen City Basketball Tournament in Buffalo in 1960. His team, Wisconsin, as well as the University of Pittsburgh squad, which included Mike Ditka of football coaching fame, stayed at the Statler. It was Christmas week and Neinas recalled that the only other guests on their floor were the girls (strippers) from the Palace Burlesk. It is easy to understand how one might remember that.

Celebrities from all walks of life stayed there. In 1962, ex-president Harry Truman inaugurated the Fitzpatrick Lecture series at Canisius College; he stayed at the Statler. Early commuters could catch a glimpse of Truman as he took his brisk daily walk down Delaware Avenue. In the 60s and 70s the Dunlop Pro Am Dinners were held in the Golden Ballroom. Leading sports celebrities of the era attended. Suites were rented out by businesses entertaining customers where they might be introduced to the likes of golfer Jack Nicklaus.

Inevitably, change set in. The Statler's stature, similar to the city itself, declined sharply as the 20th century came to an end. Much of the hotel fell into disuse. Newer hotels have taken over many of its functions. But they will never equal the grandeur that was the Statler's for much of the last century.

## The Palace; Landmark in Shelton Square
Originally printed March 2018

*Shelton Square in the 1950s was Buffalo's Times Square! A prominent place in the Square was the Palace. Talk about icons! Buffalonians, surely those over 65, remember Crystal Beach and the Canadiana. Not far behind on the list of Buffalo's icons, would be Shelton Square and the Palace Burlesk Theater.*

The bestselling Buffalo Memories Book, put together by local historian Joe Bieron, is a compilation of many of the Buffalo News stories (500 word columns) of the late George Kunz. The very first entry is about Shelton Square and the Palace. Kunz calls the Palace the "most famous Shelton Square landmark."

A decade ago WNY Heritage Quarterly did a feature on the Palace by local newspaper man, Jim Bisco. The focus was on Dewey Michaels the impresario of the Palace. Local historian Steve Cichon has written about the Palace and its place in downtown Buffalo. There is a lot of material and information "out there".

My intent is to add some color to the subject by tapping the memories of those who, back in the 1950s, visited the historic showplace.

First a few facts to place the iconic theater in its downtown setting! Shelton Square was the hub of downtown Buffalo. As Kunz notes, it was used as a place to identify your location. A stranger might ask e.g. Dick Klug, "do you know where the Ellicott Square building is"? Dick's response "you know where the Palace is, ok just down a block or so on the same side of Main street".

In the middle of Shelton Square stood the "Shelton Square Shelter"; that is where the public transit riders waited for their next connection with a trolley or bus. In the basement were restrooms, rather unsavory. As you looked around the square, you saw the "Big E", the Erie County Savings Bank Building, to the North. It was replaced by the Main Place Mall in the 1960s (some called that progress?). Looking down the street you could see City Hall. On your left stood the Hotel Niagara, a rather seedy facility by the 1950s. Nearby was the iconic St Paul's Cathedral, then back to Main Street. On the far SE corner, stood the imposing Ellicott Square Building.

Directly across from the Shelton Square Shelter, on the East side of Main Street, was the Palace block. It ran from North Division to South Division. It included several businesses including Seeberg's Men's store (buy a suit, get two pair of trousers and a turkey), a few low end establishments, a cafeteria, and Foody's restaurant (not really a fine eating establishment). But there was also the Mathias Cigar Store, the most legendary of places other than the Palace. Mathias had smokes, newspapers, magazines, and phones for placing a bet. But it was best known as a ticket outlet. There you could buy tickets for all major events taking place in the Queen City, especially Sports contests.

Close to Mathias was the Palace. Jerry Kissell, who knows as much about Buffalo sports in that era as anyone, notes that when the Palace closed in 1967, the successful college basketball doubleheader program in the AUD went downhill. He has a point there.

Why was the Palace so popular? For one thing for male teenagers in the years following World War II it was a right of passage. It was like a visit to Tommy's Shuper house where you might relieve the saloon of a hefty shuper as a souvenir, or perhaps a trip to the Crossroads restaurant where you would be dared into swallowing a gold fish in your beer.

Shortly after our high school moved to Main Street in 1950, our principal, Big Ed, warned us about heading downtown to dens of iniquity such as the Palace. Immediately lights flashed and some of us organized a "tour". Off we went to Shelton Square. We crossed the street, paid our 50 cents, and voila, we were in The Palace. The rather sparse audience, it was midday, included a few other high school adventurers, some crusty regulars, and a handful of businessmen with their fedoras pulled down over their foreheads (lest they be recognized by fellow workers). The orchestra played, the curtains were drawn, and a young lass, partially clad, paraded around and introduced the first attraction, a comedian. He was a bit corny, but funny. Then it was time for the hucksters, the pitchmen, selling Eskimo pies and boxes of crackerjacks. Each box was "guaranteed" to have a valuable prize at the bottom. We succumbed; Tim McA found an old razor in his box and immediately stood and yelled something incoherent. An usher told him to be quiet or leave. Tim sat down. Another prize was a stubby pencil. And so it went. Then it was time for a movie, B grade at best.

Finally the feature: Blaze Starr (no relation?). She performed, teasingly but actually quite modestly. She was a nicely figured, good-looking woman. Blaze was one of the three big headliners who appeared at the Palace Burlesk. The others were Gypsy Rose Lee and Rose la Rose. Other, less known performers included "Ding Dong" Bell and Tempest Storm.

We left the theater contented that we had the experience. Indeed, it was an experience shared by many teenagers of the 50s and 60s. A few examples: Chuck Wilson recalls that when pledging for a UB fraternity - his task was to visit the Palace and secure an autograph from Rose La Rose. The indomitable Chuck succeeded. Sid Warner followed up his visit, with Adrian and the Brow along, with a stop at the Gayety, a hot Jazz spot on Washington St. He ended up sitting at the bar next to Gypsy Rose Lee. Honest. He engaged in a little small talk, but no date was forthcoming.

On one of those occasions, Adrian reported that for some reason all the lights went on in the Palace (by accident?) and half of Kenmore High school was there, or so it seemed. Mike Stooch recalled that he saw Busty Russell there; she lived up to her name but that was all. Mike preferred the comedians. Roger Cree reported that he saw the "Shimmery Queen from Bowling Green." She was a disappointment. In fact he and his fellow travelers booed and hissed so much that they were asked to leave. Coach Dickerson and his Siena rifle team took in a show at the Palace They thought the experience might sharpen their marksmanship.

Tony McElroy, a Buffalo policeman whose beat in the 50s included the Palace, fondly recalls that he had a key for the back door of the Palace. The key was also used for the police call box. Tony and his colleagues kept things under control. Often they went to the basement to the Palace where they sat through orchestra rehearsals. Not bad work.

The comedians were an integral part of the show. Some future big name celebrities played there including: Phil Silvers, Red Skelton, Red Buttons, and Jackie Gleason. They were on the Burlesk circuit, just as the girls were. It was actually called the "wheel" and it operated throughout the East and Midwest. For example, Tempest Storm would sign up on the wheel and then perform at the Palace for a week, then on to Cleveland, then Kokomo, and beyond. Dewey Michaels noted that the girls were assured of employment over a 40-week period. One of the stars, Rose la Rose, as historian Tom Banchich notes, ended up retiring in Toledo.

On one rather humorous occasion, Shoes, Fring, Zuke, and myself made the trek downtown. Outside of Foodys we met a colorful character in bright Panama suit and broad brimmed white hat who claimed to be "Pete off the Pickle Boat". He followed us into the Palace. We sat near the front; Pete was nearby. As usual, the crowd was silent when the star was performing. However in front of us, an inebriated fellow started to yell for more action. Suddenly Pete stood up and hollered, "Shut up you damn nut!" Everyone started to laugh; it was just plain funny. It became part of our repertoire for years thereafter - one of us would blurt out, "Shut up etc." To us it remained just plain funny.

The fame of the Palace Burlesk spread beyond Buffalo. Back in about 1980, I was attending an NCAA convention and happened to be sitting with Chuck Neinas, the Commissioner of the College Football Association. When he learned I was from Buffalo he smiled wryly and related his only trip to Buffalo that was in 1960. He played basketball for the University of Wisconsin; his team was there to play in the Canisius sponsored Queen City Tournament that also included the University of Pittsburg. Legendary football coach Mike Ditka was a member of Pitt Basketball team. They stayed at the Statler over New Years. Neinas recalls that the only other hotel guests on their floor were the girls from the Palace. They celebrated New Years as a group. No wonder Neinas remembered.

The Palace closed in 1967. Dewey Michaels tried a new location but the

Burlesk era had come to an end. Hugh Hefner and his porn show had ushered in a new era. Playboy and its despicable offshoots permeated America. As a wise Tony Illos commented, "Current TV shows and films show more skin than the Burlesk ever did." Certainly, the long legged types who parade down the runways wearing a few inches of Victoria Secret lingerie make the costumes of Blaze, Gypsy, and Rose look tame. So does the Swimsuit issue of Sports Illustrated.

## Italian Immigrants in Buffalo
Originally printed May 2015

*PBS produced an informative history of Italian immigrants in Buffalo. Originally most Italians settled downtown and in the lower Westside, later moving to North Buffalo and then to the suburbs.*

The story of Italians in America was portrayed in a television production shown recently on PBS, Channel 17. John Maggio, whose family roots are in North Buffalo, demonstrated his expertise as a television producer putting together this excellent 4 hour special.

Immigrant patterns were similar throughout the United States. Italians came to the U.S. in large numbers at the end of the 19th century. They remained in their "Little Italy's" for several decades. Their numbers increased, they became Americanized; they began to spread out, and to assimilate.

This program got me thinking "way back when." "Hey, Zuke" I said, "when we were teenagers right after the war, where were all the Italians? Do you remember any in Kenmore?" Zuke: "They were all on the Westside". The massive immigrant waves that had flooded the city of Buffalo around the turn of the century were still pretty much ghettoized or localized at the time of WWII: Italians – Westside; Polish – Eastside; Irish – Southside. In Central and North Buffalo a mix of Jews, Germans, WASPs, and a few disaffected Irish, and some Hungarians in Black Rock. Not completely accurate, but close! In truth, there were very few Italians or recent immigrants in Kenmore in the 40s, or for that matter in areas outside of Buffalo. Obviously, that changed completely in subsequent decades. The flood of "newcomers" to other parts of the city and to the suburbs came after World War II.

Immigration has always been a subject of great interest to me. Early on,

I read Harvard's Oscar Handlin's seminal work, "The Uprooted." Handlin has been remembered for his very first two sentences: "Once I thought to write a history of the immigrants in America. Then I discovered that the immigrants were American history." At Canisius in the 50s, I had a professor who gave inspired lectures on immigrants. He, though not an Italian himself, famously said, "Thank Heavens for the Italians. Americans suffered through years of dreadful food, and then came the Italians who taught us how to enjoy good food." I used that at least a hundred times in my history courses.

Italians had come to Buffalo as early as the Civil War. Christianos settled in the Humboldt area; other Italian families in the Lovejoy district, others near Swan St., but by 1900, most Italians lived in Dante Place and in the shadow of St Anthony's Church (the mother church).

By WWII, the Italian community had moved north, along Niagara Street, and to Holy Cross and Holy Angels parishes. Connecticut Street became the hub of shopping and social life for the Italian community. Some moved further north to the upper Westside along Grant Street to Forest Avenue.

Meanwhile I had had my own experience coming to know Italians in Buffalo. In 1948, I attended high school in the heart of the thriving Westside Italian community, one block from Connecticut. (Incidentally, many Irish had lived there at the beginning of the century and a few remained, including my Aunt Annie Nellany). Soon I had new friends, Italians. Some had names I had never heard before: like Sal and Angelo, and Pat (not Patrick but Pasqual) and last names such as Marrale, Illos, Longo, and DiCaesare. With them, I smoked cigs in front of Charlie's deli, had a beer (underage) at Duke's café, enjoyed a traditional St. Joseph's table with the family of my classmate, Ange Siracuse, and learned what Marone meant. I even went to a dance with a girl who happened to be Italian (to the surprise of some Kenmorites).

Upward mobility for immigrant groups, early on, was limited to entertainment, politics and sports, (and illegally, crime). In addition to the oft-heard stories of Sinatra, DiMaggio, and LaGuardia, new Italian headliners, such as the chap who befriended Mussolini, in his early days, and another, A.P. Giannini, who headed up the Bank of America were cited.

Later, in the 20th century many Italians moved to North Buffalo. Appropriately, the Italian Festival moved from Connecticut Ave. to Hertel. Many of Italian ethnicity also moved on to Kenmore and Tonawanda, somewhat similar to the Jews who had left North Buffalo earlier for Amherst. Into North Buffalo came other ethnic groups: Arabs, Blacks, and Asians.

The immigration picture has changed significantly in the early 21st century. Italians, Poles, Eastern Europeans have become acclimated into America just as Irish, Germans and Scandinavians had done, and before them those from the British Isles, France, Africa, and elsewhere.

Americanization marches forward inexorably. We need to remember our past, the lives our ancestors experienced and the values they cherished. We should know much more than simply that some Poles bought butter lambs at the Broadway market, or that some Italians years ago brought pizza from Naples, or that the Irish did not eat corned beef and cabbage in the old country.

It is so much easier these days, via google and the internet to discover our ancestors. More people than ever are involved in genealogy quests. But it's important to place our individual histories in the larger fabric of America, to understand the common heritage. We need more documentaries and publications so we can know more about the heritage of various Americans, regardless of ethnic or racial origins.

## Buffalo's Famous East Side - Over the Tavern
Originally printed December 2014

*Buffalo's ethnic enclaves were "full" of taverns a century ago. Joe Dudzick, star Canisius College basketball player and later a Buffalo politician ran one on the Polish East Side. The family lived "over" the tavern and Joe's son, Tom, has written famous plays about life there.*

"The Play's the Thing" to quote William Shakespeare. But in Buffalo recently "the play's the thing" must refer to Tom Dudzick's play, "Over the Tavern". I saw it and it's terrific, even better than the original of 20 years earlier. For me, it was good comedy, wonderful nostalgia and solid acting. Just the right cup of tea for my generation!

I have never been accused of being a theater critic. However humility notwithstanding, I must confess to a brief acting career. Back about 1950, the CYC (me included) at St Paul's entered a diocesan-wide one act play competition (perhaps 100 other CYC's competed). We won in the first round and we kept winning, making the final four and then won the championship. That was a long time ago; the only thing I recall about the play (I don't even remember its name) was that my pal, Fring, played the part of a waiter. He carried a large tray with glasses filed with water (pretend booze) and dropped the whole thing. The loud crash caused the entire audience to laugh uproariously. We won; I suspect because the audience and judges thought the crash was an essential part of the play.

My career as a thespian ended abruptly, so did Fring's. But over the years I have maintained interest in the theater. Locally there was a time when it seemed that the Erlanger was the only theater in Buffalo; later it was the Studio Arena. Presently there is a plethora (there's a good word!) of theaters and local actors.

Back to Tom Dudzick; he is the big name in local theater now. His play captures Buffalo's vibrant East Side in the mid-20th century, when the entire area seemed to be Polish and Catholic. It was a time when it was understood that parents sent their children to the local Catholic school. In those pre Vatican II days, nuns virtually ran all the schools. Most were wonderful persons but occasionally an unbearable autocrat might appear. That's the role of Sister Clarissa, a star in the play.

The play revolves around Rudy, the 13-year-old son who questions his faith, the Baltimore Catechism and why he has to make his confirmation. Hoping to head off a catastrophe, Sister Clarissa visits the family residence and meets with Rudy's parents. Sparks fly and, well, the issue is not resolved. But there are funny lines, hilarious episodes, and some stellar acting.

Taverns were a social mecca for neighborhoods in Buffalo and similar ethnic cities in the last century. In Buffalo Polish taverns with families living above, seemed everywhere. The Irish had some – in fact, celebrated local Irish historian Tim Bohen notes that McCarthy's in the First Ward was one such place. Ulrich's, which various Eberls frequented, was very popular with the German clientele. Indeed German saloons were found all the way from Metzgers, (downtown – with its longest bar in Buffalo) to Hausbeck's and out to the Auf Weidersehn near Harlem. But the Polish were the most numerous – along Sycamore, Genesee, Walden, Broadway, Fillmore, and Seneca - all the main arteries of the sprawling East Side.

When "Over the Tavern" made its debut, I immediately was interested. The Dudzick name was familiar. Tom's brother Paul was the Athletic Director at Stony Brook (NY University), and our paths crossed at NCAA conventions. His Dad, Joe, was elected to the Canisius Hall of Fame, when I was Director of Athletics.

A segue on Joe. Big Joe (6 '11") Dudzick played basketball (of course) for Canisius College in the 1930s. He was a defensive specialist – the coach would station Joe near the opponent's basket where he could "perfect his technique of knocking shots out of the basket." The center jump also was used then – obviously, the tallest guy (Joe) could easily tip the ball to one of his teammates. In 1937, a highly rated Nebraska team was coming to Buffalo to play Canisius in the old Broadway Auditorium. The coach requested that Canisius not use the center jump. The Canisius coach was not about to give away his ace in the hole. Sure enough, Canisius won, in what the Buffalo Evening News called the "greatest victory" in Canisius history.

A few years later Joe bought a bar at 770 Seneca Street, which he operated until 1966. The Dudzick family lived over the tavern. The play itself takes place in the family residence. Tom and his four siblings grew up there. (Again, a personal note - while attending Canisius in the 1950s, I worked right across the street from the tavern, at the Motor Express Trucking Company – located between Joe's tavern and the Larkin warehouse.)

Over the Tavern is a must for anyone of Polish ancestry, in fact for anyone interested in the history of Buffalo. So is Verlyn Klinkenborg's book, The Last Fine Time, a social/family history, of the Thomas Wenzek tavern, later renamed George and Eddies. It was located at Sycamore and Herman. The book and the play are like bookends – capturing the colorful, ethnic past, of the city's famous East Side. The book is acclaimed as one of the best ever written about Buffalo (It was reviewed on the front page of the New York Times – no small feat?).

## Buffalo – Moving Forward
Originally printed December 2105

*In the later decades of the 20th century, Buffalo seemed to be a stagnant city. But in the 21st century, the Queen City has witnessed significant progress. The downtown medical complex and Harbor Place/Canalside are the best examples. Several other ideas have been suggested: some good, some bad.*

In recent years "Our Fair City: as Car Talk's Click and Clack would say, has made considerable progress. Some good decisions have been made; good ideas have begun to bear fruit.

The huge Buffalo-Niagara Medical Campus including the Roswell Park Cancer Institute, the Hauptman Woodward Medical Research facility, Buffalo General Hospital, and the new and relocated U B Medical School are great ideas "moving forward."

The reborn Harbor/Buffalo River area is a great success. Harborcenter, Canalside, The Inner and Outer Harbors - that entire area is booming. This includes Harborcenter, Canalside as well as new hotels, new lofts and condos. Even the little ferryboat shuttling pedestrians and bikers across the harbor toward the 1832 lighthouse is a great hit, as are the various Kayak launching sites.

The Erie County Harbor Development Corporation has accomplished great things. The Pedulas deserve the community's gratitude for their generous contributions, not least of which is assuring the continued presence of the Bills and Sabres in Buffalo.

Not far from the Harbor is Larkinville . Another successful example of Buffalo reborn! Between Canalside and Larkinville, more new housing is planned according to Citybration guru, Marti Gorman. Indeed her Citybration on the internet keeping Buffalo boosters up to date is another good idea.

Buffalo is indeed on the move. More ideas continue to surface. Some are good, some dumb, others mixed. It is easy to find out more about them in social media (or on non-social media) and you can read about them on the front page of the News.

Here are a few recent headliners with a few personal comments:

1. Extend the subway.  Dumb. Why spend millions of taxpayer dollars to build a subway (even if above ground?) which will have limited use? "Let them use drones," as Marie Antoinette might have said.

2. Build a 2nd Peace Bridge. Another perfectly bad idea! Just when you thought that a second bridge was a dead issue, some authorities want reconsideration.  Okay, why not also consider a third bridge, this one for bicycles? Or a fourth for horses or motorcycles! Yes, there is traffic congestion that must be considered.

3. More bicycle lanes and routes.  Mainly, a good idea. Many bikeways have been opened in recent years.  BUT, some bike lanes on some roads and city streets may be confusing and even treacherous. One may fear enraged drivers disregarding bike lanes on crowded streets; the cyclist is always the loser. There is a new green bike strip on Delaware Avenue

just past the underpass of the Scajaquada. It runs about 100 yards and the green strip changes color. Does not seem very safe!

4. Move the Canalside concerts! Not a good idea. Why kill a good thing -which would happen if the concerts were moved! On the other hand, the nearby residents have a legitimate complaint about the noise. The solution would NOT call for furnishing the complainers with earplugs or building a Donald Trump wall to seal off the concerts from the residences. But the issue should be studied by all concerned; some accommodation needs to be worked out.

5. Get rid of Columbus Day. A mixed idea! Well-intentioned people (and some politically correct nitwits) have raised this issue. Columbus, like Napoleon, Andrew Jackson, General Patton, along with many other historic figures, had flaws. That does not preclude them from being honored. Columbus was in many ways a product of his times. He also was a superb seafarer. Perhaps he should be honored in a way that Portugal honors its seafarers. In Lisbon, facing ocean-ward, there is a tremendously impressive monument; it is called "Monument to the Discoveries." It pays tribute to the numerous heroic adventures of that era.

. I heartily agree that we should continue our efforts to honor the American Indian. A national holiday for the American Indian should be considered. Some states do that now. But don't call it Indigenous Peoples Day. That is just too clumsy; it lends itself to denigrating criticism.

6. New stadium for the Bills, located downtown. A good or bad idea? I say mixed. A downtown stadium might make sense as long as it is not too close so as to overwhelm Canalside. You can be totally assured that there will be widespread discussions about this for years to come. No hurry. Make sure there is plenty of private as well as public funding.

7. Demolish the Skyway. Some say no, some say yes and a third view is: demolish part of it. I don't believe they mean demolish half of it, half way up to the highest point. If that were done you could have vehicles racing up to the top and then flying off into the harbor. What a thrilling July 4th spectacle that would make. But it might not be approved by the Common Council. Save our Skyway!

8. Statues! OK, I agree this is not really a huge, controversial issue. The Tim Horton statute near Harborcenter: that is fine. The Ralph Wilson one outside of "The Ralph" is very appropriate! He made lots of money but he has certainly "given back" to many worthy causes. There is a new statute of Teddy Roosevelt in front of his inaugural site. No one is going to argue about the significance of that. But "Shark Girl" what is its purpose?

*Big Joe's famous saloon on Elk Street, Site of popular play "Over the Tavern"*

*Inside Big Joe's – below the Dudzik's home*

*The Buffalo Skyway spanning the Harbor, Buffalo's tallest building in the background*

# Chapter 2. Around the City and Western New York

*Buffalonians and WNYers have fond memories of Buffalo's past. Legendary saloons and taverns, landmarks like the Huntley Smokestacks, ethnic restaurants, and the long-gone towpath are "colorfully" remembered.*

## The Famous Williamsville Coffee Mile
Originally printed January 2013

*Americans drink huge amounts of coffee, of every variety and price range. The first mile on Main Street in Williamsville with its numerous coffee "shops" gives ample testimony to this. In our day, it was Deco's "Buffalo's Best cup of Coffee" period.*

Drinking coffee is in. I mean - are we or are we not a nation of addicted coffee drinkers? And many Americans would walk a mile for a good cup of coffee.

I know just the place, Shangri la for coffee drinkers. It's the Williamsville Coffee Mile. Drive to Williamsville, park your car at the Sunoco station – in fact, you can even get a decent cup of coffee there. Then - For the next mile, you will find almost every conceivable kind of coffee available at an incredible number of retail establishments. The emphasis here is on The Big Five: Tim Hortons, Dunkin Donuts, Spot, Starbucks and Coffee Culture. Others receive a passing mention.

On the North side of Main St. is the Walker Center, anchored in its south-east corner by Tim Hortons, undoubtedly one of the very busiest Tim's. At 8 am - the drive-thru extends some 13 vehicles long; actually, the 13th might have its trunk sticking out precariously on to Main Street. Would it not be quicker to park, pick up one to go – you're off? Actually, the Tim servers have the system down pat – all things move smoothly - the coffee is good (but in my mind, not nearly as good as other Big 5 coffee shops).

Tim's is the dominant coffee emporium in WNY (and of course Canada). As the Fuccillo guy screams, "It's Huge, Buffalo". They are ubiquitous. They even have their own language. A guy ahead of me at a Port Colborne Tim's asked for a "double double". I asked the waitress "what's that?" She said it's Tim Talk. Tim's has an extensive menu, but their fairly famous donuts are a bit small and expensive. However the timbits are maybe just what weight watchers ordered.

Kitty corner is the Dunkin' Donuts, Number 2 of the Big 5. ("The country runs on dunkin," verse 23, book of Psalms). The parking entrance can be hazardous if there is considerable traffic on Main. It's a no frills place - small menu, few tables - a Spartan atmosphere, but excellent coffee and donuts.

Across the street, there is a McDonalds, where seniors offer up 79 cents for a decent cup of coffee. You can tell the Golden Arches is a geezer hangout, because some of the patrons are actually reading a newspaper.

Next door, another of the FAB 5, Number 3 on the Williamsville mile is Spot Coffee. The facility is something to behold; Spot regards itself as a community-oriented café – catering to every lifestyle. As you enter, you find an assortment of reading material, then the efficient counter operation with expected steep prices for special coffee and interesting food items. The dining/ drinking area – wow, at first I thought I was in the main reading room of the New York Public Library. On a recent visit there, I counted 10 tables, at which there was a computer or some electronic device at work, and most had a human in attendance. In a distant corner I actually spotted a live human being reading a book, I mean a book with pages. Honestly! Spot has experienced steady growth in WNY and has some in locations beyond – Toronto. (Shazam! It takes - you know what - to compete head to head with Tim's).

Across Main Street is a Panera's - noted for great bread, exotic sandwiches, good soup, and good coffee too. Next door is Dicamillo's bakery offering, what Judy Caserta of Lewiston calls, the best Italian bread this side of Tuscany. (They do bake bread in Tuscany - don't they?) Have your coffee with your favorite baked good!

Number 4 of the Big 5, Starbucks, is a few hundred yards away. The coffee giant of the universe suffers a bit in our area from the omnipresence of Tim Horton's. Like Spot – but not as big – the techies are there - doing their electronic thing while half-patronizing the business. Good parking but no drive thru.

Further, along Main you pass the popular original pancake house, obviously, it serves coffee. Next is Jim Grenauer's Glen Pub - good food – some coffee but better beer. Cross over Main street and a couple blocks away is # 5, Coffee Culture, with specialty teas and coffees and an enjoyable, cozy atmosphere. Breakfast served all day. A pleasant place to meet good friends!

Speaking of tea, a little shop called -Tea Leafs offers freshly brewed tea. Rather surprising that with many Asians and old time English traditional tea drinkers around there are not more places dedicated to tea drinkers. Lord, I was in Japan's Kyoto-Osaka area decades ago and felt I was surrounded by teahouses.

There you have it – the Williamsville Coffee Mile. How about this for an "original" song title: "They've got an awful lot of coffee in (Brazil) Williamsville"?

For the After 50 crowd, even more so for the After 70 crowd, the coffee scene has changed dramatically over the years. Coffee – regular - at any of the Big 5, is in the $2-$3 range. Remember "Buffalo's Best Cup of Coffee!" Decades ago that is what you were told you got at Deco's. There were a least 37 of the white and blue Deco's, usually located at the busy bus and streetcar stops. Most had a few tables, but the counter and stools were the trademark. The clientele varied: local bums were served late at night, business types and shoppers early on. And what a superb gathering place for 20 year olds to sober up after downing countless Iroquois or Genesee or Carlings Black. As for exotic varieties of coffee – no such thing at Deco's – you got one kind – whatever came out of the pot. Sometimes it was pretty awful.

*The Towpath – along the Niagara River, wiped out by NY Thruway, 1950s*

*Towpath Mayor Frank Mutz*

*Last ferryboat trip, Bird Island to Ft Erie, 1950, later docked near the Bedell House*

## Colorful Tales along the Niagara
Originally printed May 2013

*The Niagara River is the western boundary for the Buffalo area. Along the banks of that river, many Buffalonians have colorful remembrances. Some include Front Park, The Towpath, Black Rock, and Riverside, as well as the Westside Rowing club and the old Ferry Boat at Bird Island.*

Water, water everywhere, and with a harbor, a lake, and a river rushing by – there is plenty around Buffalo. Unless you have been living under the proverbial ROCK, you have noticed numerous accounts in the media about progress for Buffalo's waterfront, restoring some of Buffalo's past and offering a show place for visitors. It's a hot topic. I am adding my two cents – personal observations and recollections reinforced by information provided by geezer intelligentsia.

1. Front Park

Now that the 452 designs for a second Peace Bridge have been mothballed, serious discussion has begun concerning the approach to the existing Peace Bridge, the big plaza concept. Plans also call for enhancing Front Park, eliminating some roadways and making the park more accessible to the populace.

Also in the park is the decaying statute of Oliver H. Perry, the hero of the

Battle of Lake Erie in the War of 1812, erected there to mark the centennial. As John Kuzdale noted in the Buffalo News, "The building of the Peace Bridge and Thruway has diminished the park and left the Perry Monument isolated and forgotten." Hopefully the Olmsted Conservancy, Chuck Yeager's Café Aroma group, and all interested parties will lead the effort to relocate the Perry Monument to a more appropriate site near the head of the Buffalo Harbor. There, the old commodore would be given his due.

Of course, you cannot restore all of the past, but you can see some magnificent views of the Front, circa 1900, in Dr. Joe Bieron's postcard collection. My own nostalgia goes back to 1950 when my high school football team practiced at the Front. One warm afternoon a strong odor enveloped the area. I was quick to blame my larger teammates, Clem and especially Big Tim McA, a couple of rugged linemen. Then I found the real source - horses nearby. Yes, Buffalo's mounted police had its stables there, part of the old Fort Porter site at the Front. The horses, there must have been a dozen of them, had left their stables to do their "business" outside. Hence, the smell! The stables are long gone - so is the mounted Division, though Erie County Sheriffs still saddle up to cope with the inebriated at the Bills' games.

Benny Constantino, legendary basketball referee, lived in the old Italian community at the foot of Georgia – not far from Front Park. He recalls playing baseball near the river –the only kid who occasionally would drive a baseball clear into the Niagara was the famous Sibby Sisti.

Nearby too, for a very brief time was the Motorboat club – noted for its Dixieland music on Sundays. It was a mecca for youth throughout the city in the 1950s – as in "Let's head down there to find some good lookin' gals and have a few Jenny's."

2. The Towpath (some details – courtesy of WNY Heritage Magazine)

Granted, I haven't heard any groundswell to restore the famous towpath. However a commemorative plaque would be a worthwhile reminder of its place in our colorful history!

I am sure that the younger generation asks, "What's a towpath?" The towpath is worthy of comment. Mules had to tow the barges along the canals in the pre-mechanized age. The mules were poor swimmers so they plodded along the path aside the water. Hence – towpath. Along the canal, parallel to the Niagara River, a towpath community emerged. At one time it stretched from Squaw

Island north for several miles into the Tonawanda area. Over the decades, the towpath community shrunk and by 1950 it was centered at the foot of Ontario Street (Not far from Tommy's Schuper House, famous for its 25 pound schuper mugs). Basically the towpath community was in the Black Rock/Riverside area overlooking Strawberry Island. Sharkey Diebold's famous fish-fry tavern was nearby. Many of its patrons vividly recall the towpath community with its abundance of boat liveries, fishing clubs, bait shops, saloons and an assortment of shacks.

An old friend, Bob Warner lived on Bridge Street in the 40s. The towpath squatter community was part of his newspaper route, including Mutz's saloon, owned by the perennial mayor of the towpath, Frank Mutz. His mayoral campaigns were colorful to say the least. Anyone who bought a beer was eligible to vote. No limits. Candidates' promises included: "Beer pumps every 500 yards."

Bill Cotter, longtime head of the West Side Rowing Club, recalls the legendary "Bubble Eyes" Wagner, towpath squatter. With no sewer system, Bubble Eyes had the unsavory job emptying the waste buckets each morning into the Channel. Occasionally, after a tough night at Mutz's, his aim would be off and the waste would end up in someone's boat. Ye Gads!

Yes – the towpath was a colorful part of Buffalo's past. Hanging out on a summer evening with "nothing to do"– as youth always say, some of us would hop in a car and take the jaunt to the towpath for a little action. Indeed my pal, Shoes, was contemplating marriage with a gal from a swish part of Tonawanda. His dad commented that he might be better advised to consider a gal (wench!) from the towpath; he would be doing her a favor by elevating her status in life. He did not oblige.

3. More tales to tell - more sites to remember.

One would be the old Ferry Boat (the boat to Ft. Erie not to Grand Island). The Ferry carried cars and passengers from the foot of Ferry Street (a plaque there would be appropriate) to Fort Erie – close to where the Ming Teh restaurant now sits. The voyage across the Niagara lasted almost 10 minutes. Along with the autos, the ferry transported a host of characters. Included were racetrack patrons, who with a racing form under arm and a small tote with thermos, sandwich, and several packs of Lucky Strikes, hiked the mile from dock to track to lay down $2. (In those days, it was not uncommon for some 10,000 spectators to be at the track.) There always seemed to be some crusty geezer strumming a banjo outfitted in ripped, faded plaid shirt and straw hat –hoping his listeners (observers) would toss him a few coins. A fond memory for me - my pal, Shoes Bewick, and I took our bikes, on the Ferry to Canada, and headed up the Garrison for 15 miles to Sherkston. Much easier than the bridge!

And what about those spots further up the river, in Tonawanda and on Grand Island! Later!

## The Huntley Smokestacks
Originally printed October 2015

*The towering smokestacks at the Huntley Station along the Niagara River symbolized the massive industrial strength of the Niagara Frontier. Moreover they were used as a focal point for beach going frolickers at Beaver Island and beyond.*

Thank heavens for the Buffalo News. It keeps feeding me ideas for columns: The Huntley Station (Power Plant), Sherkston, Frog Island, the dilapidated cruise ship resembling the legendary Canadiana, and the Central Terminal. All have been featured recently.

I salivated. Nostalgia rushed through my mind. I thought back to the early 1950s sitting on the Bedell House porch with friends (Zuke, Fring, Shoes, Sid) overlooking the Niagara River (whoops, the mighty Niagara). Countless Jennys and Black Labels were consumed as we reminisced about the ol' days. Our chatter was occasionally interrupted by the cool sounds of the Stan Kenton band emanating out to the porch from the wooden Philco radio perched behind the bottles of Seagrams 7 on the back bar. At times we stopped to listen to Peggy Lee, Julie London or a Dave Brubeck number.

We looked across the Niagara at the Huntley's towering chimneys; we thought not of pollution (what was pollution anyway back then?) but of all the industry that the Huntley fed with its enormous power: Wickwire, DuPont, Western Electric (previously Curtiss Wright that had built hundreds of P 40s for World War II), Remington Rand, Spaulding Fiber (where we were all fired or pink slipped because "Shoes" kept slicing formica sheets in half, which was bad). We thought of the smelly refineries; Frontier, Ashland, Gulf and Texaco as well as Linde, Dunlop, and GM (the Chevy plant). These were places where our fathers and family members began to earn a good buck as they advanced toward home ownership, and paid vacations and became card carrying members of the growing middle class. These were places where we had summer and after school jobs. Vodra, maintained that if you failed to land a job at one factory, you simply hiked down the road to the employment office at the next one, uttered "job", "employment", or "work" and were hired. Those were heady days. We made enough money to pay our tuition, buy a used car, and afford plenty of beer.

Also Frog Island was in the news recently. Nary a soul had ever heard of it back in the 50s. We recalled Motor and Strawberry Islands. At that time there was a house with someone living in it on Motor Island - now the entire site is abandoned. Strawberry Island was remembered as where the hydroplanes (remember Guy Lombardo and George Trimper!) turned around and headed back to the Buffalo Launch Club. The island almost vanished a few years later when much of its substructure was "donated" for the construction of the Niagara Thruway in the late 50s. Frog Island is there somewhere!

Located in the same general orbit was Beaver Island. Today it is rarely mentioned; but it t was a very popular, sandy beach with good swimming back then. While wealthy Buffalonians escaped to the Canadian shore, the "Proletariat" was content with Beaver Island.

*Huntley Power Station, River Rd, Tonawanda. Strawberry Island is nearby in Niagara River*

**Penny Candy, Cherry Cokes, Thick Milkshakes and Great Comic Books**

*Cardina's – a popular meeting place for North Buffalonians, 1930s-60s*

*Del Denby at his pub, a Hertel Ave landmark*

# Old North Buffalo- With Anecdotes

Originally printed September 2013

*A century ago, North Buffalo took its place as a significant community in the city. Bennett High School and Holy Angels Academy are fondly remembered. Bustling Hertel Avenue emerged as the main business, commercial, and entertainment artery.*

North Buffalo – generally understood to be the community on both sides of Hertel, including some of Central Park and Parkside, stretching north to Kenmore Avenue, east to Bennett High School, west to Elmwood - thrived for many years.

The North Buffalo community developed about a century ago. Many changes have taken place since then, legends moved on and familiar structures were torn down. Two landmarks recently closed: Holy Angels Academy and the North Park Theatre.

But let's go way back with memories of some old timers. Bob King grew up on Frontenac in the 30s, graduated from 66 and Bennett High – he proudly states that Bennett was THE premier Buffalo public high school. The graduate rate was near 100 % (in fact who kept score – it was assumed everyone graduated). Probably 90 % went to college, many to premier institutions: King and Hal Bergwall to Brown, Myron Hunt to Middlebury, Dick Munshauer to Cornell. King recalls that the only thing Bennett could not do was defeat Kensington in football.

The North Park Theatre was the place to be for teenagers. After the movie, it was across the street to Percy's which Helen Reilly remembers as the premier ice cream parlor of the era. She also recalls spending countless hours at the North Park Theatre. No TV in those days so whenever a new film arrived at the theater, Helen was there to preview it. Meanwhile Helen's future husband, Wayne, patronized the Everglades, a block away. Helen is of the famous Cardina family that operated the general store across from the Zoo's entrance. Cardina's, too, was a mecca for youngsters, especially those on the way to the Zoo. In their later years, they turned their loyalties 3 doors away to the Park Meadow.

50-60 years ago the Park Meadow was a Cole's type saloon, a magnificent "hangout." Jim Burke is the unofficial historian of the Park Meadow. Jim was there (in fact Jim was on both sides of the bar) when Albert was the chief bartender, when Stofer owned the place, when Bob Lawler was behind the bar, and when Dennis Brinkworth became the owner. The Meadow ranks as one of the most memorable places in North Buffalo. Same goes for the Everglades. But there also was Andy's, formally Andy Atkinsons- where, if you could reach the bar, you were served. A bit later, there was Tony Bafo's saloon, the Chez When. In the 40s Bafo's downtown bar was a late night hot spot for musicians and show people who stopped over from the Town Casino, a stone's throw away. Tony moved to Hertel when the downtown nightlife went South. On the wall were photos of top entertainers of the bygone era. During the infamous Blizzard of '77 – when the city was shut down – all regular traffic was prohibited, but the Kloepfers, George and John, recall seeing a police car pull up in front of the Chez When. Out stepped Tony Bafo- saying, "only essential services can be open – What's more essential then the neighborhood saloon." Tony Bafo – one of the good guys.

The Everglades- now there's a bar that should qualify for the registry of historic places, like a Toot Shors in New York or the Brown Derby in Hollywood. I doubt I ever encountered an old timer who did not have a fond memory of the Glades. That is where Jackie Jocko began his nightclub act right after WWII. Yes – that same Jackie – who is still pounding the keyboard and belting out the old lyrics at E B Greens in the Hyatt.

George Wilcox flew airplanes over the Pacific in WWII, and returned to claim a spot at the Glades, often joining his sister Mary Lou and her fiancé, Tony McElroy. Three regulars: Joe Scully, Mike Davis, and Jerry "Klu" Soltys, separated by thousands of miles, corroborate the story about the night the canopy over the bar came down engulfing a number of serious beer drinkers, including Scully's pal, Bill Wiedeman. No one was hurt but a few draft beers were seriously impaired.

Joe Scully calls the NP Theater the entertainment center of North Buffalo – every kid who had 3 cents was there on Saturday afternoon. Afterwards, of course, Percy's was the place to be. If you got bored, you could meander down the block to Summit Hardware and watch TV in the front window. Few people owned television in 1950. The Friday night CYO dances at St. Margaret's were also extremely popular. Blossoming musicians like Mark Ruslander and John Corr got their start there.

Mike Davis, Bennett '53, Canisius College some years later, remembers the Friday night drill: to the movies, then off to Atkinsons, corner of Hertel/Main. 10 cents a beer and great beef on wecks were featured. A few years later, Mike, discovered the Everglades, befriended Chet, Wanda, Eddie, and Helen – the proprietors.

Soltys, Bennett '52, logged many Saturday afternoons in the NP Theater, watching the serials. His favorites: Hopalong Cassidy, the Lone Ranger, and the Green Hornet. He recalls the streetcar picking him up daily in front of school 21 and taking him to the end of Hertel to Bennett, sometimes stopping so he could pick up his favorite Gertude Shalala's chocolates.

In the mid-50s the Colony was the place to be on a Sunday afternoon. No – not THAT Colony, but the one that featured Dixeland music. Joanne Callahan even met her future husband there, Mary Manzella sang, and Ann Littlefield danced the day away. Everyone enjoyed the Dixieland music on Sunday afternoons.

If Sunday was party time, then Monday meant, for many of the coeds from North Buffalo, a return to school at Holy Angels Academy. Ever since the Academy had moved from West Avenue to Shoshone in 1930 many of Buffalo's leading females had graduated from there. Now it is no more.

But the memories survive. If there is any one person who is identified with Holy Angels it is Sr. Jean O'Shaunecy. She was there almost from the beginning. Sr. Jean was born about the time the school opened, grew up in North Buffalo, graduated in '50 and stayed there into the new millennium. No one was more representative of HAA. Hundreds, even thousands, of HAA alumni recall St. Jean (aka Doc) with admiration, respect and affection. Dorothy Higgins McNicohlas, circa '65, says "She was a wonderful ambassador for the school."

On occasion, Sr. Jean had competition. When the HAA seniors got close to graduation, Checkers became an attraction. What other high school had a bar so close, virtually an annex of the academy, much to the distress of the Grey Nuns!

A few blocks away, many of those same young women worked at The Sample Shop. Indeed Tony Maggiotto claims that HAA girls never cashed their paychecks, they simply turned them back to the store to cover their many purchases.

There is much more to be told. Characters abounded: Coach Jim DiFasio, Archie Lee, the grizzled old chap who hawked the Courier Express up and down the avenue, Leroy and his flag decorated tricycle, and more.

All neighborhoods change over time: some for the better – some head downhill. North Buffalo remains solid.

# Historic Taverns/Legendary Bartenders
Originally printed March 2012

*Every generation has its favorite watering holes (taverns, bars, saloons, gin mills etc.), usually personified by a legendary bartender. People go, to paraphrase the ditty introducing the popular "Cheers" TV program of the 1980s, "where everyone knows my name."*

There is a buzz about town that Kevin Godzich, (Adams Rib) and Tom Harkens (professor emeritus, Circle of Thieves) are under serious consideration for the National Bartenders Hall of Fame. They would be joining a very elite group.

Lest one think I jest, allow me to note that bartenders and their work place –the local tavern- have played a very important role in America since colonial days.

Anyone who has visited Colonial Williamsburg might recall the famous taverns there, especially the King's Arms on Gloucester Street. Perhaps George Washington did not sleep there but he surely imbibed there, as did that rabble rouser Patrick Henry, one of the earliest denouncers of the tyrannical British. Colonial taverns were valuable sources of news as well as sites of secretive meetings prior to the American Revolution. They helped to unite the colonies against the Redcoats; they played an important role in the founding of America.

In the War of 1812 Wilson's Tavern on Lundy's Lane (Niagara Falls, Ontario) played a vital role. At the commencement of the battle of Lundy's Lane, one of the last great battles of that war and the biggest on the Niagara Frontier, the proprietress of the tavern, the widow Deborah Wilson, dispensed hospitality as well as crucial military information. She informed General Scott of the size and equipment of the British troops hiding in the woods nearby. The Yanks were successful.

At the end of the 19th century, Teddy Roosevelt rounded up his famous Rough Riders at the saloon in the Menger Hotel in San Antonio. Off they went to Cuba in the Spanish American War of 1898, with the future President leading the charge. Incidentally a short time later Carrie Nation of anti-saloon league fame, took her ax to the Menger bar.

The significance of taverns (saloons, bars, grills, gin mills, watering holes, restaurants, pubs, inns, etc.) went far beyond wartime.

By the early 20th century, corner taverns were ubiquitous in all major cities. They played an important part in the lives of recently arrived immigrants. They served as a place for political gatherings, where aldermen could be hand-picked, graft (all varieties) purveyed, future mayors nurtured and voters rewarded. Bars continued to be places for the exchange of general news, and increasingly for sporting news. In the age before telephones and radio, sports fans gathered to find out how their favorite baseball team fared. Throughout the day, scores arrived via telegraph, and were promptly posted on the bulletin board. Later that evening, a boxing bout (John L. Sullivan!) or wresting match might be held in the backroom. Of course betting on virtually all sporting events was commonplace. Early sporting saloons were predecessors of some of the grandiose sports bars of today, minus the 498 large screen TVs and 23 flavors of vodka.

Buffalo had its share of ethnic saloons. George and Eddie's on Sycamore Street, the subject of Verlyn Klinkenborg's classic book, *The Last Fine Time*, was an outstanding example of an ethnic bar. A touch of that past – still resides in Ulrich's, known as the oldest existing tavern in Buffalo. Check out the fading photos and political posters and you get the flavor of local politics of many decades ago. Jim (son of Hoops) Daley runs the place; his German-born mother gave it the "Kraut" flavor.

There were many others: Joe Dudzik's (stage play – "Over the Tavern") on Swan, Early Times in South Buffalo, McCarthy's in the Ward, and Nucherino's in Riverside, and of course the Roundtable, a stone's throw from the Statler, with Big Jim Naples presiding. Later Naples had his own saloon on Ledger Street – very unpretentious but he once hosted George Steinbrenner and his NY Yankees. Naples loved to refer to himself as the local Toots Shor's after the legendary owner of the celebrity hangout near Madison Square Garden in NYC. Another prominent old time bartender was Bob Lawler, initially at the famous – or infamous -Park Meadow, in later years at the Saratoga. After having been away quite some time I popped in and Bob said, "Still drinking Genesee?" A good memory - that's part of what makes a memorable bartender.

I would be remiss not to mention other youthful watering holes. The Golden Pheasant and the Kenmore Tavern (from the porch of which 7 of us, during the Korean War period, left to serve Uncle Sam), the Bedell House on Grand Island, the Fort, Whitey's near Canisius, Gleason's near State, and the Everglades (Mike Davis presiding) on Hertel. Was there any time left for school? Or work?

The old taverns were wonderful places, but it was the bartender that made a place special. The best were men of dignity, of class. They were respected, virtual pillars of the community. Typically they wore a white shirt and tie, did not tolerate rowdies, and frowned on obscenities and "dirty" talk. They knew the regulars by name; even those who patronized the place infrequently were recognized. The customer was made to feel important. Bartenders knew when to listen, when to comment and when to keep a distance. They developed a special sense of selective hearing.

Despite changes in recent years some good professional bar men remain. Louie Leone and Mike at Oliver's (even if Louie does parachute off the bar on New Years' Eve) are first rate. Mike McPartland (you get a barrister when you befriend Mike) and his relatives are top notch at McPartland's Corner. Hertel Avenue has the Wellington Pub - Kim Hazelet did such a terrific job running the bar that she became the CEO.

Mike Herzog, a Wellington Pub original, moved on to join Big Bruce and the celebrated Tommy Morrissey at Morgan's. They were a terrific trio. The Place had Joe Broc and Tom Gabbey; Jim Grenauer is establishing his claim to fame at the Glen Park Tavern in Williamsville. Mike Thomas at Checkers is properly renowned. Del Denby's was a special case with either Del or the late Hubie operating the taps. Old timers also recall Joe Lang, Donny Pappas and Art Ponto at Cole's. And on and on; WNY has had no shortage of hospitable saloons manned by capable bartenders. Who, of the After-50 crowd, could forget Archie of Duffy's Tavern – "where the elite meet to eat" or Joe the Bartender, aka the unforgettable Jackie Gleason, or Sam at Cheers "where everybody knows your name"?

Tom Harkens and Kevin Godzich - two of the best in the business. Harkens (now retired) has that glowing Irish mug – it lets you know that you were going to be served a good drink (along with a little lip if he liked you). Kevin is almost magical at keeping all customers satisfied at his busy bar. His wealth of sports minutia puts him in good standing with John Rogers and other distinguished Rib intelligentsia. Harkens and Godzich meet the stringent criteria for the Bartenders Hall of Fame (even if those qualifications have not been codified).

*Hall of Fame Bartenders Kevin Godzich and Tom Harkens*

*Enormously popular restaurant in downtown Snyder*

## Ethnic Restaurants – 60 years ago
Originally printed December 2013

*In the 1940/50s ethnic restaurants in Buffalo were limited in number. There were a few Italian eating spots, as well as the occasional German, Polish, or Irish restaurant. The only Chinese one I recall was Chins. Today numerous ethnic restaurants of every imaginable variety are found, right here in Western New York.*

I ate at a Burmese restaurant recently with my grandson, Joey, for his birthday. He said it was his favorite restaurant. My Lord, when I was his age, the only thing I knew about Burma was that there was a road there- the famous (or infamous) Burma Road in WWII over which General "Vinegar Joe" Stilwell traveled to fight the Japanese ("Japs" as they were called in politically incorrect days). We ate at the Sun Restaurant. Halfway through my meal (I think I had Amare Thar Hin), it dawned on me that globalization is upon us in a big way. The evidence: Even in a midsize city like Buffalo, there are, in 2013, many good ethnic eating places.

I got to thinking about ethnic restaurants in the 1940s and 1950s. Were there any then? Did we even know what ethnic meant? Now, to phrase it as President Nixon would have, let me make it perfectly clear- I am not a good expert or "foodie." I even liked the SOS in the army. I was a chowhound, not a connoisseur. I make no pretenses of being a professional restaurant reviewer of the Janice Okun or Andrew Z. class. This column simply recalls some of the good ol' ethnic restaurants for the "After 50 plus" generation.

Six decades ago, there were not many ethnic restaurants. In fact, there were far fewer restaurants, period. People just did not go out to eat as they do nowadays. They could not afford it and often there were too many kids to feed. Going out to eat was a big occasion, like to celebrate an anniversary, a signifi-cant birthday, or a First Communion. Now, DINKS (double income – no kids) do it all the time; many others do it often.

The recent Burmese excursion reminded me that I could only remember one Asian/Chinese restaurant in Buffalo 60 years ago- Chin's. It was near down-town, on Main near Virginia. It was a long narrow place, resembling a diner. I recall my Dad saying, circa 1948, "We are going to get some chop suey (it was that or chow mein- limited menu) at Chin's!" I used to think, "What's Chin's?" When we arrived at the restaurant, I overheard some lout (again, not politically correct today) say to his kid, "That's Chin leaning on the counter; he's a Chinaman." Actually, Mr. Chin was Americanized. At Thanksgiving time, his menu featured several turkey selections.

That was my early Asian (ethnic?) experience. Today, at last count, there were some 4,390 Chinese restaurants in WNY, not counting the strip in Fort Erie. We also have several Japanese and Thai eating establishments. Back in the 50s, who had even heard of Thailand? We knew it as Siam, from the Broadway hit "The King and I." Remember Yul Brynner, the King, dancing all over the place in "Shall we dance – dum dum dum…"

Buffalo did have large ethnic sections in the 1940s and 50s. There was the Irish in South Buffalo, the Polish on the East Side, and the Italians on the West Side. Central and North Buffalo had Jews and many folks of British and complicated French/Germanic ancestry (Alsatians?). There were a few others too. I recall that Hungarians had an enclave in the Amherst St./Grant St. area where the St. Elizabeth (patron saint of Hungary) Church stood. Lackawanna had a variety of Eastern Europeans, including a number of Slovaks, Croats, and Ukrainians. Blacks or African-Americans did not arrive in large numbers until World War II and, at best there were a handful of Hispanics. Indeed, I don't even remember that word used then. Some Puerto Ricans were brought in to do the bean picking in North Collins. That was seasonal.

It was true that ethnic neighborhoods had numerous corner saloons but as far as distinctly ethnic restaurants that served fine food some 60 years ago, there were few. One that stands out was the legendary Polish Village located on Broadway across from Sattler's. It was noted for entertainment as well as food. Big Steve and his Polish language radio program originated there. The accomplished accordion player, Ray Manuszewski, performed there too. If St. Stan's was the mother church of Polonia, then the Polish Village was the mother restaurant of Polonia.

The Irish were not celebrated for their cuisine. Remember the old joke about the seven course Irish meal? (Answer: a potato and a six-pack).

On the other hand, the Italians were always noted for good food. But again, unlike today, there were not many Italian restaurants back then, Santora's on Main Street and Lorenzo's on Pearl St. come to mind.

Laube's Old Spain, a Buffalo landmark on Main close to Shea's, was Spanish only in décor. Seafood was its specialty. Not far away was a Lebanese restaurant, the Cedars of Lebanon. Passersby would stop at the front window to watch a lamb (or something?) slowly roasting on the rotisserie.

Then there was Canadian cuisine! Across the Niagara River was the Queens hotel, another legendary place! A Canadian meal there consisted of a block of Canadian sharp cheddar, crackers, and plenty of O'Keefe's ale (also a few Cincinnati Creams- remember the clear, white bottle?)

Two outstanding Buffalo restaurants were Victor Hugo's, an exquisite French restaurant on Delaware, and the Park Lane with Peter Gust Economou at the helm. Though the owner was born in Greece, Greek cuisine was not conspicuous at the Park Lane.

The Germans fared a little better. There was Troidl's in the Kensington area, which later begat Scharf's in Schiller Park, as well as Schwabl's, Carl Meyer's Hof, and Ulrich's. They all deserve mention.

Today, the demographics have changed significantly. The Irish still maintain their dominance over South Buffalo, but the Polish, save for a few octogenarians, have vanished from the East side, escaping to Cheektowaga and West Seneca. The Italians left the West side, migrating to North Buffalo and on to Kenmore and Tonawanda. The Jewish have moved to Amherst and many of the other "old stock" have disappeared into second ring suburbs. New immigrant groups have arrived, countless ethnic eating places have opened, and that has to be the subject of another column.

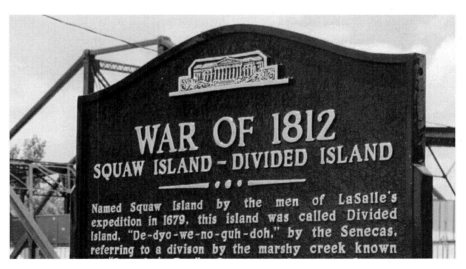

*War of 1812 Memorial, Squaw Is. – now Unity Is.*

# The New Squaw Island
Originally printed March 2015

*For many years Squaw Island was a rather isolated place at the south end of Bird Island, just past the International Railway Bridge. Because of objections to the name "Squaw," the island will be called something else in the future.*

## DEYOWENOGUHDOH

What's that you say? You don't recognize it!

So we have this challenge handed to us from Councilman Golembek - change the name from Squaw to Deyowenoguhdoh. The easy way out would be to just drop the squaw and use D +13 (total of14 letters!) Thus a sign stating "Squaw Island Park" would be replaced by "D + 13 Park" Nah, D + 13 – won't work. Too drab!

I turned to local authorities to assist me. WNY Heritage consultant Jacek Wysocki, Chemistry Professor turned local historian Joe Bieron, and renowned authority on antiquated downtown properties and the entire Black Rock area Frank Eberl. Each of these experts provided valuable information about Squaw Island. However any errors or misinformation you detect in this column are mine alone.

Squaw Island is at the north end of the strip of land bordering the Black Rock Channel or Canal. The South end is Bird Island, once the site of the legendary West Side Rowing Club that burned down back in the 70s. The Bird Island pier (Break wall) wends its way much further north - under the Peace Bridge and almost to the Buffalo Harbor. It is a grand place for a walk.

Being an inquisitive cub reporter I drove down Niagara Street. Staring right at me as I neared Tonawanda St. loomed a big painting on the railway overpass: "Welcome to Squaw Island." And to think that I had recently been saying that few people had ever heard of Squaw Island! Wow, Mayor Brown and his sign painting staff are really something. I proceeded about 75 yards, turned right and came upon a plaque indicating the entrance to Squaw Island.

The plaque mentioned both "Squaw Island and Divided Island." It also noted that the island was divided by "Marshy Creek" known as "Smugglers Run" and that Squaw Island was the site of the burning and sinking of the British warship, HMS Detroit, in the War of 1812. Finally the plaque indicated that in 1679 the men of Robert De La Salle's ship named the island: "Squaw". Must have been a few squaws hanging out there back then?

I drove along the one lane parallel to the International Railroad Bridge. A Border Patrol officer in his SUV sat guarding the end of the International Bridge. Obviously he was ready to prevent illegal immigrants, terrorists, potential pot growers, and dangerous elements and malcontents from entering.

At the end of the one lane, you either take a left to enter the sewage- aka waste water treatment plant or proceed a little further turn right, go under the railroad bridge and there it is! Squaw Island Park! I drove around the island; the road is replete with the customary pot holes (hey! winter in Buffalo!). There also was a trail and some recently planted trees but little else to indicate much of a park.

A segue for "After 50" readers who are at least 75. The entrance to Squaw Island is very close to where Tommy's Schuper House once stood. The Schuper House was a Buffalo landmark in a class with the House of Quinn, or the Park Meadow. Young drinkers from all over the city had to stop there at least once – it was a rite of passage. It was similar to swallowing a gold fish in your beer at the Crossroads Bar on Harlem near Wehrle.

At the Schuper House, you drank beer, usually Iroquois or Simons, out of a hefty glass, "the Schuper." I mean that thing was a lethal weapon. It was a big thick glass bowl on a thick stem of glass. It seemed designed to be a souvenir. You just had to have one. You either paid the $1.00 or, like Zuke, hid the Schuper under your jacket. I actually think that the proprietor expected to "lose" several Schupers each night – the price of doing business. And of course the Schuper would eventually end up on your bedroom dresser collecting matchboxes, dust and coins. Then when you left the nest a few years later, your mother would toss it out, just as she would your faded AAU insignias and assorted sports pennants, and an unused Crystal Beach ticket for the Comet.

One more thing about Deyowenoguhdoh Island! The new signage as well as park improvements may be a problem for us downtrodden taxpayers who are getting ready to be fleeced for a new football stadium. There may be a solution – right there staring back at us from the Squaw Island plaque: The citizenry enlists top legal talent to commence a class action suit (grounds - politically incorrectness) against the French sailors from LaSalle's ship for naming the island Squaw back in 1679. (How long is the statute of limitations? Are any of their descendants still around?) The entire area could benefit.

Finally the entire area of the new park could be part of the revival of Canalside. I'm thinking mainly of races. Yes, races involving crews from the rowing clubs, and also motor boat races and perhaps kayaks, actually almost anything that floats. If all that water froze you could even have ice skating marathons, like on the Rideau Canal in Ottawa. The races would start at the D +13 park docks and head up the channel under the Peace Bridge, past LaSalle Park and eventually into Buffalo harbor, ending up in grand tumultuous fashion at Canalside to the cheers of thousands and to the surprise of additional thousands of concert goers awaiting the arrival of the Goo Goo Girls or whatever the latest hot group is these days.

# Chapter 3. The Good Ol' Summertime in our Area

*The older generation has cherished memories of such legendary places as Crystal Beach, the Bedell House, as well as summer campsites, old swimming holes like Mike's Pond, and the Windmill Point Quarry. Lerczak's and the Canadiana will never be forgotten.*

## Summer Watering Holes - 50- 60 years ago
Originally printed August 2011

*The shores of Lake Erie have always been a popular destination for the young people of Western New York. Back in the 1940s-60s, no area was more popular than the Evans/ Angola beaches. And no site there was more popular, than Lerczaks. The iconic Lerczaks! It became legendary. No superlatives can do it justice. It was THE place to go.*

A recent issue of Gusto in The Buffalo News highlighted the popular summer spots of 2011. It might seem like "all Greek" to the After 50 generation. The 20 somethings are enjoying Mickey Rats, Captain Kidds, The South Shore Beach Club, and the Dock at the Bay; watering holes strung along the American shore of Lake Erie. Unfamiliar names for 70 year olds but that same area, Angola, Evans, Sunset Bay, evokes memories of our youth.

The drive out to the lakeshore is certainly quicker now with the skyway and wider highways. Back then you traveled over the Ohio Street Bridge, out Fuhrmann Boulevard, past the massive Bethlehem Steel complex and its 42 neighboring saloons. You might be held up for an hour if the bridge were up

– meaning that a lake freighter was passing through the canal on its way to Donner Hanna Furnace and Republic Steel (a tedious wait, alleviated only if Zuke or Tony Evans had remembered to bring a couple of six packs). Once you past Hoaks and Foits seafood restaurants the rest of the way was quicker.

What were the hot spots of 6 decades ago? There was the Inn at Sunset Bay, a large beer palace on the beautiful sandy beach. It was especially busy on Sunday afternoons as patrons listened to Jazz, Big Band, and Dixieland wafting over the beach. Many pleasant cottages surrounded Sunset and Hanford Bay. Ten miles closer to Buffalo was the Point Breeze Hotel, aka Sneaky Pete's. Where did that name come from?

The main focus of summer fun was the Evans-Angola beach area. Four main saloons/bars stood ready to serve the thirsty. The South Shore Inn was especially popular with the South Buffalo guys and gals, like Dick Robinson, the Curtins, Crowleys, Kulps, Connors - many of the Timon/Mt. Mercy types. And then at the other end of the quarter mile strip was Jimmy Goodrich's, an upper class restaurant, run by the Hall of Fame boxer of that name. There you had two choices, behave and enjoy your drink in rather refined ambience or be obnoxious and then be tossed out, literally, into the night. Don't mess with an ex-prize fighter. Next door was the colorful Bill Miller's "Riviera", known for its famous patio plus its second floor rooms that could accommodate those who had too much to drink and needed a bed for the night. Not a 5 star rating but who knew.

Then there was Lerczak's. I mean, talk about legends! Old timers think of: the Canadiana and Crystal Beach, of the Everglades and the Town Casino. But Lerczaks! It stood alone. Over the years it developed a mystique.

The basics: It was a good sized log cabin. An oblong bar served about 60 - three deep; adjoining it was a large drinking hall that held perhaps 150 imbibers, maybe more, with throngs waiting to get in.

Lerczak's drew its patrons from all over Western New York and beyond. Ray Manuszewski, WWII Marine, remembers going there with his East side pals from the Polish American Youth Organization. He smiles: saying it obviously sounded subversive and was probably on Sen. Joe McCarthy's hit list. Ray claims that none of his pals were card carrying commies.

At the door, you were proofed, a draft or sheriff's cards sufficed – (often forged). Once inside, drinking was the order of the day. Carlings Black Label was the brew of choice. Hey Mabel, Black Label! Iroquois was second, Simons,

Kochs, and Steins, followed. Remember these were the days before the affluent generation began consuming chocolate martinis and a Blue Moon white grain beverage pretending to be beer.

Integral to the Lerczak legend was owner-proprietor, Ma Lerczak. Bob Farringer and Jim Burkey recall that she navigated the floor in search of those in need of a beer. Buy one or leave was the name of the game. Ma in her red knit sweater, her all season uniform, seemed ubiquitous. She was ably assisted by her good looking daughters, Ginger, Evelyn, Eleanor and Ann. Who said feminists did not have clout back then?

If a Lerczak addressed you by name - you were "IN". You strutted around like a big shot, coddling your brew, hoping that less fortunate patrons would say: "Hey that guy knows one of the Lerczaks." Mike Davis of North Buffalo, a regular, claims that even Clyde the dishwasher knew him by name.

The bar/drinking hall was bursting with vitality. In today's jargon, the place ROCKED. The popular songs were sung over and over again: patrons moved about freely belting out the lyrics of I love Paris, Sh Boom, and hits by Patti Page, Kay Starr (no relation), and Rosemary Clooney.

For a place packed with hearty drinkers there was surprisingly little trouble. Occasionally there might be some turmoil in the parking lots, boys will be boys, jealously feuding over a well put together blonde. Larry C. remembers a famous bout (McDuffie-Bartok) that simmered near Lerczak's, broke open on the Ohio Street bridge, and reached its bloody finale in the Deco parking lot in Kenmore. But back at Lerczak's things were always under control, due in no small part to the bartending corps. In order they were the Lerczak sons, off duty State troopers and Canisius football players.

There is much more to write about the Lakeshore of that era. That will come later.

*Overview Lerczak's Restaurant, Catholic Church, Connors Hot Dog stand and Ma Lerczak's home*

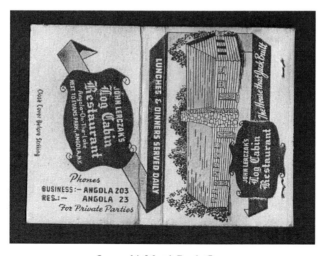

*Lerczak's Match Book Cover*

*Main Ballroom with ubiquitous Jukebox - Lerczaks*

## The Old Swimming Hole

Originally printed July 2014

*Before suburban homes had backyard pools, kids found swimming "holes" in a variety of places. In the Snyder environs, Mike's Pond was popular. The Kensington pools (at Grider) beckoned to youth from all over Buffalo. Beaver Island and especially the Bedell House on the Niagara River were Kenmore/Tonawanda favorites as was the Windmill Point Quarry across the bridge in Canada.*

Some local pundit one once said; it might have been Jim Kunz or maybe Adrian Voyer, that WNY has more backyard swimming pools, percentage wise, than anywhere else in the nation. Hard to believe! But even if true, it was not always that way.

60-70 years ago - it was a totally different story when it came to finding a place to swim.

For Kenmore youngsters, circa 1940, it was the Mang Wading pool - not surprisingly on Mang Avenue almost to Military Rd. Actually it was precisely at the Horse Path (later named Melrose Rd). Horses had used it a few decades earlier; as a reminder, old stagecoaches remained piled up behind the public works, not far away.

So Duggan, Watson, Bork, Grimmer, me and our siblings would hike the few blocks to the pool. Shoes Bewick would come from the other direction. Our mothers cautioned us - if the water is dirty - stay out or you'll get Polio. Dr.

Salk had not yet perfected his miracle vaccine. Polio was the big fear in those days. Indeed we did know some victims. Mang Pool was fairly large. Frequently it was dirty, its corners would accumulate a variety of vile items: assorted garbage, tissues, orange peels, a royal crown bottle or two, even an occasional discarded lampshade. Some infants were not toilet trained – no wonder the water reeked. Occasionally the pool was cleaned – it would be safe for a day or two.

A few years later we ventured forth in search of other "swimming holes." The best may well have been the diving and swimming pools at Kensington and Grider. In those days, city workers did a pretty good job keeping them clean. You HAD to take a shower (usually ice cold) before entering the pools. Teenagers came from all over North Buffalo and the near suburbs. We rode our bikes which were usually still there when we finished our swim.

Another place to which we either biked or hitchhiked was the Bedell House on Grand Island. Now there was a legendary site! Before the Grand Island Bridge opened in the 1930s, islanders took a ferryboat from the Bedell House to the mainland. By 1950 the ferries were outdated; one of them, the Orleans, found a resting place along the Niagara shore about 75 yards south of the Bedell House. The Bedell House itself was a grand old rickety structure, an old saloon/hotel. It rented rooms on the 2nd floor in the old days. The first level had a beer hall/dining room with typical long wooden bar bearing countless carved initials. The floor needed work: the uneven boards made you feel you were walking the deck on an oceangoing ship in turbulent seas. A screened wrap around porch, despite wobbly tables, time-worn chairs and warped floorboards, was a huge attraction.

A few years later, our athletic activities gave way to beer drinking on that magnificent porch. Sitting there with a cool Genesee or Iroquois on a warm summer afternoon you could enjoy the beautiful scenery, and occasionally watch the likes of Guy Lombardo or George Trimper in the hydroplane races on the Niagara.

Flush with the porch was the dock. It was about 5 feet above the water; the pilings rose another 3 feet- so if you dove from the pilings it was an 8 foot dive. Could be risky, given frequent flotsam in the water! I once hurt my back trying to avoid debris and swore off diving forever. My pal, Fring, said it probably did not hurt my chances for the Summer Olympics.

The dock and the ramp leading down to the water were in decent shape; however you had to watch out for splinters on the warped planks and an occasional rusty nail. The entire structure would not have survived inspection by government agencies.

The water, at its shallowest, was about 6-7 feet deep, way over the Brow's head. You HAD to know how to swim or you learned quickly. Swimming in the Niagara was simply delightful. Often we swam over to the Orleans. Signs on the ferryboat stated boldly: "No trespassing," which we promptly ignored. We jumped off the upper decks again and again. Sometimes we swam up to Daverns then floated back down to the Bedell House. Dangers abounded. There was always the chance that someone might drown in the fast moving current of the Niagara. We all survived.

Across the river in Buffalo was Riverside Park with its popular swimming pool. The park was a welcome oasis in what was then a pleasant, albeit modest, workingman's section of the city. The park led right down to the river (the thruway did not exist then). The waters of the Niagara beckoned to the Riverside residents including the Warner brothers, Gary and Bob, who frequently threw caution to the wind and swam out into the current to the buoy marking the entrance to the Black Rock channel. Bob, later a hall of fame swimmer, recalls that the swift current could easily take you downstream to Motorboat Island.

Meanwhile other local youth were enjoying Mike's Pond. The pond was actually one of several quarries in the Williamsville area just off Main Street where the I-290 would be built in the late 1950s. Many quarries were filled in but Mike's Pond survived and did so in an almost primeval setting. It was surrounded by woods, trees and thick underbrush. It's still there, and measures about 100 by 50 yards. Mike's Pond beckoned to teenagers from miles around who were looking for a place to cool off on a summer afternoon. Buffalo resident Joe Bieron biked there. Bob King of Snyder and longtime Harlem Road resident Bob Baus were regulars. So was young John Gaglione – who years later became Pastor of Christ the King Church. Rev. John swam; he did not walk on water. He remembers the sand beach at one end of Mike's Pond. Jeff Genrich, whose home now abuts the pond, confirmed this. Jeff indicated that his father, Willard, who had built the Landmark Lord Amherst hotel, provided the sand.

Another legendary swimming "hole" for area youth in the early 1950s was the Windmill Point Quarry. It was easy to enter Canada in those days, so on a steamy afternoon, we would pile into Elmer Arnet's '37 LaSalle, with Vodra (Double D) riding shotgun, and head for the international border. As we approached Canadian customs, Moe demanded we light up our Luckies or Camels so as to provide a smoke screen thereby fending off the swarms of sand flies that were part of the welcoming committee upon entering Canada.

Windmill quarry was a superb place to swim. No one seemed to own the place; it looked like – well, an old abandoned quarry. It was never crowded. We parked, actually abandoned the car, climbed up on a few rocks, dove in and swam in the refreshing waters.

Alas, the old swimming "holes" are long gone, changed beyond recognition, off limits or just not the same. The Bedell House burned down in 1988. Sad! Windmill quarry is now inundated with campsites and surrounded with impregnable fences. Pools in private clubs and in backyards are ubiquitous. New municipal and community pools have been built. The affluent, and even the not so affluent, have second homes on the Canadian or American shore with access to beaches. (OK, the public beach at Crescent is only 15 feet wide?)

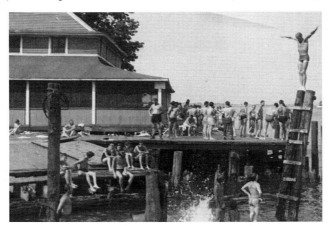

*Bedell Dock – Beware planks with nails!*

*Windmill Quarry – 2000. A remote swimming hole in 1950's*

# The Canadiana, aka Crystal Beach Boat
Originally printed September 2016

*The trip (10 miles) to Crystal Beach aboard the Canadiana was literally a rite of passage for the youth of Western New York in the decade following World War II. After 1956, the boat went elsewhere. It returned eventually to dry dock in Port Colborne where it languished then disappeared.*

We have all heard much about Crystal Beach and the Crystal Beach Boat (CBB), aka the Canadiana. Nevertheless, I added my two cents about the legendary beach and amusement park, and herewith my additional two cents about the equally legendary boat.

Ah yes! It was awesome; at least that is how a youngster viewed it! On my maiden voyage, in 1940, I was filled with anxiety. I mean going to a foreign country across what seemed like the Pacific Ocean. Mom and I boarded the ship from behind the deteriorating Dante place projects. I rushed to the third deck for a good look around a very busy harbor; tugboats huffing and puffing, a grain ship being pushed down the Union Ship canal, a few freighters towed here and there. Nearby the Detroit boat, (twice the size of the Canadiana) was waiting to take passengers to the Motor City. Alongside the harbor, trains were unloading coal. Other trains were leaving and entering the D L & W terminal.

"All aboard", the Canadiana chugged slowly out of the harbor, picking up speed as it passed the first break wall. It was time for me to spend a few minutes on the first deck looking through the screens down at the massive engines. They thumped away so vigorously that I swore we were on the Queen Mary. Also on the first deck, not far away were some guys playing slot machines. Young Tony Illos watched them in a trance, anticipating future trips to Vegas, yes, slot machines in the 1940s on the Crystal Beach Boat.

Back on the second deck my mom sat with some friends in the plush inner cabin amidst the brass railings and mahogany trimmed panels. Then up to the top deck to gaze in awe at the pilot house where the captain, a rather grisly old seafarer, guided the ship like a veritable Chris Columbus on the open sea. Eventually we came upon the initial sightings of our destination. First the Cyclone (to be replaced shortly by the less perilous Comet), next the Ferris Wheel, and soon we were docking at the long concrete pier. We disembarked, hurried through. Customs "Where were you born?" – that was all, and off we went for hours of frolicking.

We caught the 9 pm boat for home; the return voyage was mysterious. It was dark. Would we ever see land again? Alas, off starboard some red lights on towering radio transmitters from Hamburg are sighted. A sure sign that land was near.

The Canadiana cruised past the historic 1833 light house. The final thrill was to watch the 215 foot ship turn around in the harbor and dock so the bow is once again facing out toward the clear blue waters of Lake Erie.

What a grand ship! It was remembered primarily for trips to Crystal Beach. But it also was cherished for the Sunday evening cruises! Three hours out in the lake tripping the light fantastic, on the largest dance floor on the Great Lakes, to the mellow sounds of the famous (locally anyway) Harold Austin Orchestra.

The 1956 season was the last for the Crystal Beach Boat. An incident that year involving Black and White youth, many called it a race riot; some preferred to regard it as juvenile delinquency, led to the ending of the CBB trips. Indeed Dave Costello, a frequent visitor from Elmira, recalls that rowdy behavior encouraged by excessive beer consumption, became more frequent on trips that summer than in previous years. Moreover boat trips were increasingly less profitable. The great American automobile love fest was underway in the 1950s; many resort seekers preferred to travel by auto over the Peace Bridge for a quick 9 mile trip up the Garrison Road to Shangri la. Another factor was the increasing competition from newer amusement parks.

The Canadiana was headed for an uncertain future. In the 1960s it was docked on the Cuyahoga River in Cleveland where it sank (briefly), was refloated, and eventually made it back to Buffalo by way of Ashtabula. It never became a seaworthy passenger ship again. Valiant efforts were made by various individuals and ad hoc groups to raise money and secure grants to save the Canadiana; hopefully to restore it to its former grandeur. Ed Patton was part of the group that wrote a grant to save the CBB, but, unfortunately the CBB was in Canada and so the funds could not be applied.

By the end of the 1980s, the Canadiana settled in Port Colborne, at the Marsh Engineering Works. The CCB was docked in a small slip, just off the Welland Canal, directly facing the Robin Hood Flour Mill. There it languished until its bitter end. In 2006 the Crystal Beach Boat received its death notice. Pay up or move. The steam engine was saved and made it back to the U.S. What was left of the hull, the wood and steel, was disassembled for scrap.

It its final years, I frequently stopped by to see how the once proud vessel was deteriorating. The photos above indicate stages of deterioration.

I later showed my grandsons the photos. Nick Hassett thought the Canadiana may have been hit by Japanese dive bombers while tied up at Pearl Harbor. Joey Hassett surmised that the Canadiana was used in the invasion of Okinawa, the last great battle of WWII and ended up being a target of a Japanese Kamikaze.

Of course the truth was much less dramatic.

But what wonderful memories remain - the legendary SS Canadiana, its dock; indeed, the entire industrial and commercial complex that made Buffalo one of the busiest inland ports in the entire country has been replaced by numerous marinas housing hundreds of sailboats and powerboats. Also, on any given day, one may observe 94 kayaks floating around the harbor. Some of the paddlers are getting their daily exercise; others are looking around in sheer wonderment, occasionally listening to the booming rock groups at Canal Side. Hey, it's all part of the rebirth of Buffalo.

*Final days of the Canadiana, 2000, in Welland Canal*

*Sad – Canadiana ready for scrap heap – 2012*

# Crystal Beach – What Again?!
Originally printed July 2016

*Someday Crystal Beach will be only a footnote in local history. For most of the 20th century, CB was huge in the life of Western New Yorkers. It remains so in the memories of those "After 50."*

Crystal Beach and its appendage, the Canadiana: so much has been written about this topic. Local bookstore shelves are loaded with CB/Canadiana publications. Many convenience type stores also carry WNY historical items, which invariably include CB/Canadiana material. Much of it is trivial, even hokey; occasionally some is pretty good.

Just when I thought nothing else could be said about Crystal Beach or the Crystal Beach Boat; it happens. Mary Kunz Goldman had a fine piece in the news recently: "Reflections on Crystal Beach". Her father, George penned superb pieces on WNY's past, his daughter now follows suit. Channel 17, WNED-TV chimed in with "Remembering Crystal Beach Park." It was far superior to other previous programs telling us about the CB/Canadiana.

I cannot add much, just some personal reflections. Mary Kunz Goldman (MKG) notes two murals, the Canadiana and an old coaster, on the wall at the Ridge Road Tim Hortons. Actually you can find similar photos hanging in stores and restaurants throughout our area, a fitting testimony to the staying power of the subjects. The best I have ever seen hangs in a condo in Pompano Beach, Florida, the home of Owen and Sandy Doyle (nee Hall). Sandy is a child of CB as the Hall family ran Crystal Beach and the Canadiana for many years.

And who can forget the famous Hall Suckers. Sandy made the cinnamon ones. On Sandy's condo wall is this massive aerial photo (1940s) of the entire CB Park. The view extends from the stadium complex at the Eastern end (where on Kenmore day, Zuke, Trouble, and I would grovel in the sawdust for shinny pennies) across the amusement park itself (showing the Cyclone) and over to the sand beach and crystal water, then northward to the legendary Loganberry stand. I was mesmerized by that aerial view. After time out for Owen's famous shrimp scampi I would return to more gazing of the striking aerial view of Crystal Beach Park.

Today, Crystal Beach is more and more a distant memory for many. Indeed anyone under 30 (CB closed in 1989) was never there. On the other hand those of us over 60, recall the glory days.

One feature of the Ch. 17 production, that previous programs often neglected, was the Cyclone. OK, it was dismantled 1946. Nevertheless, as a little squirt I managed to sneak in under the height sign, standing on my tiptoes and took the terrifying ride. It was far scarier than the memorable Comet that replaced it. Oh if my mother had only known.

Most publications ignore some of the legendary park rides; they may not have been sensational but they were timeless and legendary including the Caterpillar, the Hey Day, Flying Scooters, Roll-a-Plane, Old Mill (find a nice gal and try a little necking) and the Wild Mouse. Most do note the Giant Coaster, Magic Carpet and Laff in the Dark. The sugar waffles are always mentioned. Sid Warner and Adrian ate them by the dozens; they always made me sick.

The dance hall, aka the Crystal Beach Ballroom! Both MKG and CH 17 highlight that memorable edifice; the dance floor was enormous. In the early 1950s, my cronies and I were regulars there; the Big Bands were still in vogue. We all loved Stan Kenton and his singer, June Christy. They "rocked." Kenton's Peanut Vendor and Jump for Joe (in honor of local DJ Joe Rico) were show stoppers. Woody Herman was also a favorite. We stomped our feet with the best of 'em, while the Brow and Blue Devil Cole pursued the pretty young gals. What great times!

In the years that followed, our children too enjoyed Crystal Beach, each with a favorite memory. A yearly trip to CB was a must, rivaling the annual visit to "The Falls". That reminds me of my very first trip to Crystal Beach. It was in 1940; we lived in Depew. Mom, my brother and I, walked, carrying traditional webbed picnic basket, to the train platform near Transit and Walden. We boarded the train; the train ride itself was a first. My brother exclaimed: "Did you see that huge steam locomotive?" We alighted at the massive Lehigh Valley terminal on Lower Main Street across from the newly constructed Memorial Auditorium, walked the short distance to the Buffalo Harbor dock, boarded the majestic Canadiana and set sail on what seemed like an endless ocean voyage. Upon arrival in Canada, we hurried past customs ("where were you born?"). The rest was pure ecstasy.

I cannot leave the subject without mentioning forays to Sheehans and the Derby. Of course, that was years later. O'Keefe's was the favorite back then, not Labatts or Molsons.

*Cyclone coaster (pre-Comet) at*
*Crystal Beach 1945, a most*
*terrifying ride*

# Our Farmers' Markets Overflow with Wonderful Produce
Originally printed October 2012

*The Niagara Frontier is blessed with many farmers' markets. Among the best: the one in North Tonawanda and the one in Port Colborne, Canada. Of course, the Broadway Market was legendary in the 1940s.*

There are markets and then there are farmers' markets. I am a market expert, at least in my own mind. My wife and I have had a long standing agreement. I do the grocery and market shopping and she buys cars, appliances and furniture. It has worked quite well.

Our area is blessed with many farmers' markets. My top picks are North Tonawanda and Port Colborne. First, a little historical perspective! Markets go way back, as far as the Hanseatic League of European cities, probably further - to the Greek and Roman times. Maybe even the Garden of Eden would count - - let's let that pass. Whenever farmers had extra crops, they looked for a way to sell them, and when towns and cities grew, the citizenry had to eat, so they turned to farmers markets.

My own market days go back to the 1940s. The "after 65" generation can relate to this. My mom took me to the Broadway market. Oh, I know as soon as someone mentions the Broadway market they think of Easter hams, and butter lambs – a once a year phenomenon. Well I mean the Broadway market in its heyday. Back when newly arrived immigrant families shopped there daily. Many "old" families joined them.

A trip to the Broadway market was entertainment for me. While my mom shopped for the necessities of life, my brother and I checked out the live animals. There were always puppies and kittens, and chickens too. What a memorable sight to see an old woman in babushka point to a hen. The farmer would grab the hen by the legs, tie it, and give it over to the woman for a few crumpled bills, who would then stuff the hen in her shopping bag. She headed home on the Broadway streetcar, performed the chicken's execution, plucked it, then into the pot for supper. There were also rabbits and ducks at the market and occasionally a pig, goat or lamb could be spotted. I don't recall seeing a cow – Jack of Beanstalk fame had taken care of that.

In the 60s I became a regular at the Clinton-Bailey Market; that was the big one then. It is still there but not like it used to be (well, what is!). In the past few decades the North Tonawanda market is the place to be. On a typical Saturday from late spring to early fall some 40 stalls are in use. Many farmers and several vendors, most from Niagara County display wonderful fruit, vegetables, plants, and flowers. Once in a while a guy selling wallets or sunglasses or Rolex watches (reduced from $10,000 to $20) makes an appearance.

A few of the regular merchants: Jim Jones from Newfane and Steve Kroph also from the same area and Carly and her 99 year old grandfather Elmer from Pendleton/Wheatfield. Others deserve mention, such as John Susite of Ransomville. He and his family operate a large corner section of the market. Dan's produce, down the row from John, has a bustling business with plenty of family involved. And then there is Tina, the cheese lady. Tina has good cheese at good prices, but she's often so frenzied on Saturday mornings just trying to keep family members running the business smoothly or digging around in her truck trying to find the Havarti or Limburger, that she has little time for small talk. But Tina is there year-round; I am sure she has time to kibitz on a bleak Saturday in March. And the blueberry lady! I mean if you want the most delicious blueberries this side of heaven, you go to her – right across from Elmer. She brings her berries all the way from Olean.

This time of the year, apples flood the market. NPR recently reported that there are now some 7000 varieties of apples in the U.S. Not all are at the NT Market but many are. Remember when you were a youth – it was either a Mac or a Cortland, that was your choice. Now there are Gala, Rome, Jonathan, Empire, Crispin, Honey Crisp, and on and on. Bob Butler, native New England apple authority, claims that the WNY apples are the best in the nation.

Up in Canada, 20 miles from the Peace Bridge, the Port Colborne market flourishes on Fridays in the summer months. As many as 35 local farmers display their produce all neatly arranged to form a veritable blaze of colors. Such an appealing scene would be worthy of a painting by Monet or Cezanne. Mary Hilborn, is just one of several hard toiling farm women who come to market from all over southern Ontario. Included too are Mennonites from the small congregation in Stevensville and also some Quakers.

Welland, Ontario has a large market on Saturdays, somewhat similar to Port Colborne's, but also features a number of butcher shops. Reminiscent of the Broadway market, a variety of languages are heard, notably Hungarian, Italian, several East European tongues, and, of course, (it is Canada) some French.

Markets abound. Some really don't rate. A guy, masking as a farmer, sets up a table with some peppers, peaches and a bushel of tomatoes. Nearby a lady sells a few jars of jam. They call it a "market!" Actually most of our local markets are first rate – just like our summer weather. Nice coincidence. A major asset for our area.

*Joe Scully at the Kroph (Steve and Brian presiding) stall, North Tonawanda Market*

*The N T Farmers Market: Elmer Moje (103 yrs) and granddaughter Carley.*
*Elmer first came in 1920s in horse and cart with his father*

*Retired Engineer, Jim Jones at the Market*

## Summer Camps
Originally printed July 2010

*The number and variety of summer camps today, especially sports camps, is astounding when compared to the handful that existed a few generations ago.*

Maybe what is needed is a "camp for camps", perhaps a three day pre-summer event to help parents and kids decide which camps are best for their situation.

At last count there were some 300,000 summer camps offered in the United States – many of those in Western New York. That may be a little hyperbole, but there really are a huge number of camps available.

It wasn't always like this. Remember the good ol' days! Actually some of those days were good and some were not. Camps were few. Most kids I knew attended summer scout camp for a week when they reached the age of 12. Camp Turner in the Alleghenies, St. Vincent DePaul and the Lutheran Camp Pioneer on Lake Erie were also available as were 4-H club/camps (after all, every city slicker needed a taste of farm life). The YMCA and YWCA and the Camp Fire Girls also held summer camps. Not much else. A few kids from families with more disposable income might find their way up north to a canoeing camp in Algonquin Park. Sport camps, however, were virtually nonexistent.

Kids played sports in their own neighborhoods. In the 1940s baseball was king. The talented kids might play on some midget team; they were the exception. Most of us had to settle, literally, for sandlot ball. Here is the way it went. You got a glove, probably a Christmas gift, autographed by Chet Laabs or some other local hero. One of your pals produced an old ball sufficiently wound with electric tape and a bat, chipped but not cracked. The neighborhood boys gathered at the corner vacant lot, (sometimes a girl joined, commonly referred to as the tomboy). You moved the rocks out of the infield, established a rough location for the bases and home plate, chose up sides and then played until your mother sent a sibling to fetch you for dinner. On some days you might go for the big time and play on the manicured lawn of a nearby church – until the Reverend found out and ousted you.

Then the great growth of suburbia took place. Housing developments popped up like dead fish on a torrid summer day on the shore of Lake Erie. No more corner lots for ball games. And the sports craze began to sweep America. More sport camps were essential. They began to proliferate; there is no end in sight.

The Buffalo News publishes a full listing, and there are many similar listings in the various local weeklies. There are camps for every conceivable form of human activity; reading, writing, and arithmetic as well as music, painting, ballet, theater arts, and more. Many deal with computer and technological endeavors.

Every sport has its camp, though I am not sure about curling. I did hear that somewhere near Winnipeg, Manitoba a curling site is being developed. (I mean, let's get ready for the next Winter Olympics). Horseback riding is popular. You never know when there might be a job available what with the renewed interest in the historic Pony Express. Tennis and golf camps abound. If a 6 year old shows any promise, the old man might send him to Florida when he can avoid the normal schooling and just concentrate on golf in anticipation of being the next Tiger Woods (on the golf course, of course ).

Basketball camps are all over the landscape, everywhere there is some vacant pavement. In the James Naismith tradition a peach basket is placed on a pole and a camp is organized. It's inexpensive – there always is a plentiful supply of local college or high school coaches ready to join your staff. You sign up a few dozen of the local youth for a few hundred smackers each, give them a t-shirt, a box lunch and a basketball, toss out the ball and let them play, A little instruction along the way makes them feel that they are getting their money's worth.

The basketball camps vary; some can be quite good. Avoid the ones that feature big name speakers; those celebrities don't contribute much except their name.

Some sports camps border on the absurd. You don't just have football camps for offensive and defensive players but you also have them for quarterbacks, kickers, and receivers. And you can find a camp for linemen who want to run a 40 yard dash in full gear better than anyone else. In baseball, there are plans for a camp that caters to left handed pitchers under 5'4" tall who suffer from obesity but have avoided all childhood diseases, other than mumps.

Summer should be fun for kids. Choose wisely – you are only young once. Our youth should be exposed to different activities, pursuing them with kids of different backgrounds and with different interests. Young people will specialize soon enough in their lives. Encourage them to attend that sport camp that really appeals to them, but also to spend some time at a more general one.

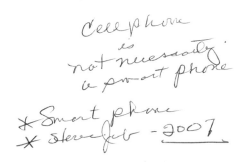

Cell phone is not necessarily a smart phone

* Smart phone
* Steve Job - 2007

# Chapter 4. Senior Citizens: A Much Different Generation

*Visit favorite coffee shops and lunch places around the city and suburbs, and you will find lots of senior groups reminiscing, about the good ol' days, that set their generation apart from today's youth.*

## Cell Phones and all that "Stuff"
Originally printed March 2011

*Cell phones have become ubiquitous. But for the After 50 crowd, it was an entirely different world in terms of communications back in the decades following World War II.*

Remember the new "stuff" available 60-70- years ago: frozen food, portable radios, and electric phonographs instead of wind up victrolas. Ah, how far we have come today.

Communications is the most obvious area. Cell phones have become an almost indispensable part of life. Hard to believe but I first used one in the early 90s. The occasion was a football team from Dortmund, Germany was visiting Buffalo (watched the Bills' practice, attended Canisius sports events, and played against some local German soccer teams) and I was the host. The German in charge had a cell phone, the size of a shoe box. He taught me how to use it – I was intrigued.

Improvements came rapidly and now we have virtually weightless mobile phones that can do everything except fry an egg. A case in point: recently my 8 year old granddaughter, Kate, looked at my cell and asked why I did not have grandma's birthday on it. I said, authoritatively, that it is a phone, not a date book. Less than a minute later she had logged in to calendar and entered grandmas' birthday. Shazam, as old Captain Marvel would say – I was startled.

So Kate and I talked about phones. In the old days, (isn't that always how the Over 50 generation begins) when I was your age, we did have a telephone. It was black. Just like Henry Ford's famous model T, you could have any color you wanted, as long as it was black. The phone had a rotary dial, with a cord resembling a python. Actually it was a vast improvement over what my own grandfather had. He lived on a farm and if he needed use of a phone he had to hitch up the horses and head to the general store 6 miles away. Then he had to "ring it up" just like in the old Buster Crabbe movies.

In the 1940s, we had our own phone at home with our own number – a 6 digit one – I still remember it – DE (Delaware) 2509 and it was a party line.

Kate's eyes lit up – "you could party on it?" - No – not that kind of a party. Party line meant that there were other phone customers, usually neighbors who used the same telephone line. You might be talking to a friend and hear a click - it could be that busy body, Gert Bickerton, 4 houses away listening in on your phone conversation. Kate said that must have been fun – I said no, just an early case of invasion of privacy. She was perplexed. She asked about calling relatives who lived far away, like Aunt Jen or Aunt Kate. Of course being a typical grandparent I could not resist telling her a "war" story. When I was in Korea in the 1950s, the soldiers would have had to travel from Munsan to Seoul (32 miles on dirt road), and then wait in a central phone station while a bunch of operators tried to make proper connections. It would take an entire day, few had the time and the money ($72 did not go very far). So it was usually an agonizing process limited to dire emergencies.

Kate was almost speechless. If phone use was so limited, how did anyone find out anything, like what was going on in the world, what were my friends doing, who won what game, how did I take photos? I interrupted, I used to have a little Brownie - 127 film camera, took black and whites, "2 by 4" and Nixon's camera shop had them developed in a week. She took the cell and did something with it and said "I just took your picture." I was dumbfounded. Virtually instantaneously, a phone that takes pictures! She asked if I used Facebook. I said that we had never even heard of that, or smart phones, IPhones, IPods, IPads, internet, computers, twitters and all that electronic stuff. I could tell she felt sorry for me.

I said Kate - in my day the sources of information were the newspapers and the radio. With a puzzled look on her face, she stated that a newspaper is something that remains in an orange wrapper lying in a corner until trash day. For those over 50, Kate figured the newspaper was simply a source for finding  out who died. Partly true, newspapers are getting thinner and scarcer and many have gone the way of downtown retail shopping.

We ended our talk discussing the perceived advantages of cell phones. She said you can use cells anywhere, while driving (even if illegal) and in restaurants, churches, movie theaters and you do not have to talk to anyone face to face. I admitted that I had observed young people in crowds each using a cell and total-ly unaware of other human beings nearby. Depressing? I have seen a woman in line in the supermarket on the cell discussing family issues. Anyone could listen in, and she could care less. What happened to privacy?

Well that is life on the fast track. Or as Walter Cronkite would say: and that is the way it was 60 years ago and is today in 2011.

## Arise, Get Your Coffee and Meet Your Friends
Originally printed September 2015

*People are retiring earlier and living longer than ever before. Retirees find a number of ways to use their extra time in a worthwhile fashion. One popular way is to meet friends, for coffee, for lunch or just for a "little something." Medical experts claim that the important thing for the health of these retirees is that they are socializing.*

What do retirees DO? Do they do anything productive, or do they sit around watching TV and reminiscing about the good old days (old, but not always good!) and then doze off? Actually, many retirees keep amazingly busy.

Women seem to cope well with their "golden years" by spending time with family, gardening, making blueberry pies, playing bridge, and reading best sellers. They get involved in church activities, volunteer at food pantries and hospitals, and care for stray pets. There are countless ways to get involved. Then, there is exercise. Look around; the landscape is dotted with exercise opportunities. There are a zillion fitness clubs – places to swim, pump iron, or hop on the elliptical or treadmill. There are fun runs and marathons- 5Ks, 10Ks, 20Ks, and even 100 mile events; as well as kayaking, bicycling, and hiking.

If you retire at 60, you may still be able to run at 65, jog at 75, and walk at 80 (shuffling along your walker). You can still do some sort of exercise.

As for the male members of the species; they do many of the same things as women. But men are much more conditioned to socialize than women, as photos will attest. Women seem more content than men to be left alone for periods of time.

Guys get together for lunch or for coffee. They enjoy "shooting the bull," or, as 87 year old Butch Wilcox says, "tell some of the same stories (often white lies) over and over again." These often involve Crystal Beach, Lerczaks, Sunset Bay, the Bedell House, the Palace Burlesque, and, of course, retelling their athletic exploits. The latter seem to grow larger as the passing days make them increasingly difficult to verify. Current events are not neglected; the momentous questions of the day are discussed, including ISIS, Iran, Obamacare, climate change, the Bills and Sabres, and, "How much tip should we leave the waitress?"

From 9:00AM through early afternoon, you will find men (and a few women) in groups of 2-10 having coffee or lunch at any number of places.

Decades ago, when retirees were fewer, these gathering sites were not as numerous. Cardina's across from the zoo, was a legendary meeting place. Another I recall was a general store at 7th Lake in the Adirondacks with traditional cracker barrels amidst a few broken cane chairs. Once, I tried to participate but was ignored because I was too young. The store was close to the Loon Saloon. What a great name for a drinking establishment!

Nowadays, you will find these social gatherings all along Sheridan Drive, on all busy neighborhood avenues such as Hertel, Elmwood, and Union Roads, on Main Street in East Aurora, Main St. in Williamsville, and Main St. in the University District. They can also be found in fast food establishments: McDonald's has good, inexpensive coffee. Some prefer Tim Horton's and doesn't virtually every busy corner have a "Tim's?"

As for Starbucks – sorry seniors, that place is off limits unless you are carrying an iPad or laptop!

*The Regulars - Coffee at the Café Aroma, Left to right: Yeager,
Mancuso, Warren, Dave Costello, Mike the Blogger, Big Tim*

*Fallon class of '52 at Brunner's, Left to right: Clark, Zorn, Brinkworth, Vic Marrale
(foreground), Clem Eckert, Klug, Tony Illos, Dicesare*

*Famous Four: Smitty, Clem, Starr, Fring*

## Generation Talk
Originally printed June 2014

*We hear much about the Greatest Generation and the Baby Boomers. But those who came of age in the 1940-50s sometimes feel neglected. They are the "in-between" generation. They deserve more attention.*

There has always been talk about generations. Usually it's the older generation lamenting the antics of the younger set, as in: "Why don't they do things the way we used to?" or "What's wrong with those kids, anyway?" That probably has been going on since the Garden of Eden.

More recently we have heard much about the Greatest Generation. Tom Brokaw popularized that phrase in his pretty good book with that very title, "The Greatest Generation." It focused on those who came of age during the Great Depression and then served in World War II. Some 16 million served in the armed forces but virtually the entire nation of 140 million were in some way involved in the heroic effort to overthrow Hitler and the Japanese Militarists.

Their era is coming to a close. Although this very month the Greatest Generation will again be in the spotlight as the country celebrates the 70th anniversary of D Day. As every American knows, that massive cross channel invasion was the beginning of the end of the conflict in Europe.

Nowadays we find an emphasis on the baby boomer generation, that cohort of Americans born in the years between 1946 and 1964. Many baby boomers became the leaders in the most turbulent decade in American history, roughly from 1965 to 1975. Those years were marked by momentous changes: the birth of the Women's Lib movement, environmental concerns, the sexual revolution, the drug culture and especially the anti-Vietnam war protests and the Civil Rights struggles. When that generation tired of protesting, new generations arrived and proceeded to make headlines. The past 40 years, have witnessed Generation X, Generation Y and now the Millennials.

But we have not heard much about the generation between the Greatest and the Baby Boomers, those born in the period of the late 1920s to the 1940s. They are now the senior citizens who are rapidly replacing the Greatest Generation.

Sometimes that group, especially with reference to the 1950s, was called the silent generation. Silent! Well, compared to the following decade – Yes. Indeed the noise from the 60s is still being heard. Actually the 60s had strong roots in the 50s, especially the Civil Rights Movement. Of course this underscores that there is inevitably some overlapping from one generation to the next.

Perhaps those born between the Great and the Boomers could be labeled the "in between" generation. They came of age in the postwar decade and shared the values and culture of the Greatest Generation. They were patriotic; willing to serve their country, witness the Korean war (100,000 casualties and 33,000 killed). They were a church going generation - it wasn't until years later that church attendance fell off significantly. Men and women dressed "up" as in the past, wearing suits, ties and dresses as the occasion warranted. You would not find some bozo showing up at funeral in baggy jeans and a muscle shirt. Everyday language was fairly polite; obscenities were limited to the barracks and locker rooms.

The "in betweeners" were products of the Great Depression. They did not suffer as some of their parents did, but the hard times did influence their young lives. They learned to care for things and not waste. Admonitions like the following were common: "Don't' waste food, clean up your plate." "You want new shoes? - you have ONLY been wearing that same pair (for school, church, and play) for two years." "What do you mean, you don't want meatloaf again - we only had it twice this week." "Your sweater has a hole in the elbow and it has been patched three times – okay then we will see if your older cousin has a hand me down."

As for World War II! Only a few extraordinary events might be remembered by the "in between" youngsters: Pearl Harbor, D Day, the Atomic Bomb, and certainly the tremendous jubilation at V-J Day. Nevertheless the war, like the depression, had a pervasive influence on the "in betweeners." All sorts of things were collected: scrap metal, alumni foil, lard, candles, all directed toward helping the war effort. The "in betweeners" might remember old guys serving as air raid wardens, aunts becoming "Rosie the Riveters" and uncles and older brothers as casualties on Okinawa or at the Bulge. And if the youth mowed a neighbor's lawn or shoveled his snow, those nickels and dimes would go toward buying a $25 war bond.

This "in between" generation matured in the late 40s and 50s. Their music was basically the same Big Band Era sound of the Greatest Generation; Benny Goodman, the Dorseys, Ellington, and Glenn Miller. They entered high school and college, married (someone of the opposite sex), had children, and went on to enjoy life in the half century long period of unprecedented prosperity in America. Heavily influenced by the Greatest Generation, they were often able to better adjust to the prosperous times than were many of those who matured toward the end of the millennium.

One thing the "in between generation" lacks is an adequate understanding of modern technology: iPhones, iPads, Facebook, the internet, texting, twitter, etc. Thus, reliance on the much younger generation is vital.

# Geezers, Gays, and Changing Lingo
Originally printed July 2013

*Language can be confusing. Euphemisms are plentiful. Political correctness adds to the confusion. Words that were acceptable years ago are now taboo. Comedian George Carlin is a master at addressing the problem.*

So Zuke says to me "this English language can really get confusing:" - double meaning words, euphemisms, figures of speech-, "especially when the politically correct screwballs make noise."

I mentioned that he ought to read George Carlin, no stranger to the screwball category. Carlin calls political correctness, "that playground of guilty white liberals." Zuke liked that – despite his 50 years as UAW activist.

Carlin wrote some classic material about language and especially euphemisms. For instance, we no longer have old people in the US; now they are senior citizens, golden agers, mature adults and even the pre-elderly. Personally, I lean toward curmudgeon, codger, and geezer. I think geezer is a "cool" word; it's more colorful than the others. Buffalo recently hosted the Golden Ager games. Would not "Geezer Games" have sounded better?

The late sportswriter Larry Felser used the term geezer occasionally but that is not where I first came upon it. 60 years ago the Tonawanda Parks Department was run by a chap nicknamed "The Geezer." Nothing malicious, just an old guy! If you wanted a choice summer job, you went to the Geezer. Tending to the Sheridan golf course, while being paid, and getting a great suntan so that you could dazzle the Kenmore dollies to boot, now that was an enviable job. Sy the Fly and Phil Morey had jobs there. My pal, Zuke and I wanted the same. We headed to the parks office, marched in, and that's when I made my first mistake. I let Zuke do the talking. Zuke addressed the secretary (these days called an administrative assistant) saying he needed to see the Geezer about a job. "Who?" asked the secretary? "The Geezer, the head man." Standing right there was the "Geezer" himself. He glared at Zuke and informed him he was not getting a job – period. He looked at me and said "you too, you're his friend." We were shown the door but not before Zuke let fly some earthy zingers.

We have countless euphemisms. Check the food business. We don't have waiters or waitresses, we now have servers. The dishwasher - is now the utensil sanitizer. I wonder if you advertised in the Bowery in NYC 50 years ago how many poor people would answer a help wanted ad for: "utensil sanitizers" instead of dishwashers. As for poor people, Carlin notes that the Lord always preached about helping the poor. But poor people don't exist anymore. We now have financially disadvantaged. They do not live in slums but occupy substandard housing. They are not on welfare, or, God forbid the dole, but rather on public assistance. A euphemism, sounds so much better; I mean even the Wall Street plutocrats receive public assistance. Ah - the wealthy – on the dole.

And think of job titles. No more store clerks, now they are product specialists. A suit salesman is a wardrobe consultant. Associate is now a big word - sales associates. All those kids tossing you burgers and fries – they are associates. Walmart has thousands of these job titles. How about a shoplifter being called a "cost of living adjustment specialist" Terrific!

Secretaries do not exist anymore. Recently a sign in Wegman's, near where all the local farmers' produce is piled, stated: "do not forget 'National Administrative Assistants Day" – which, I brilliantly deduced had now replaced national secretary's day.

Another word that has become quite common is groping. Presently it has something to do with improper sexual contact – mostly males toward females. Our military men have recently become infamous for groping activities. 60 years ago, it had no such meaning that I am aware of. Groping then meant trying to find your way. My pal Smitty could not see very well in the dark – he became an excellent groper in Sheas' Kenmore Theater – trying to find an empty seat.

Groping – sex – it figures. Society has become obsessed with sex. Male, female, transgender, transvestites, gays, lesbians, homosexuals, gay pride, live-ins, significant others, life partners - they are all part of the mix. Now we have to be concerned about not offending anyone with almost anything we might say. How about the word gay - has that ever evolved??? Years ago I worked with a DP (slang for displaced person – no PC police then). We were dock wallopers at Continental Can. The DP, aka Vodra – came here from Eastern Europe following the war (the Big One) and was anxious to learn the language. I gave him an American history text. Years later, I saw Vodra and he said he was confused about our first president. He read that George Washington was having a gay time at some governor's ball in colonial Virginia. Was he a Gay Man? I said he was gay but not a gay man, gay does not exactly mean gay anymore - and we parted ways.

How about this one! A Notre Dame Football star was "tossed" out of school for making a "poor academic decision." Back in the old days, Stuart Barcik was tossed out of my grade school for being stupid. Or was it just plain dumb?

A cowboy is now a cow person. Okay kids: let's play cow persons and Indians,. Whoops. I mean cow persons and Native Americans - unless those Indians are from Canada - then they are Native Canadians or?

I was admonished recently when I saw a short guy and called him a midget. I was told that that person was vertically challenged.

If I don't end this column – I might be "word challenged!"

## A Senior Survey
Originally printed January 2015

*This survey is directed to those who remember the decades 1940-1960. It asks about people, places, and events of those years.*

New Years' resolutions – they're everywhere: But not for me! None this year! Last years' were all broken by February. Instead - a survey. I know surveys are also regular features in community newspapers. And most are predictable and boring. How often have you seen: the favorite local sports team is "Da Bills", or favorite Chinese restaurant is Ming Teh (highly overrated) or favorite beef on weck is Charlie the Butchers (again overrated).

But this survey will be a little different. It features responses from seniors – most over 75. The margin of error is – well not exactly 3-4% but about 80%. The survey deals with the 1940-60s time period. Thus Taylor Swift does not qualify as a response nor does Justin Bieber.

Here goes:

1. Who was the most popular female singer of the 50s? Dave Costello and his Café Aroma friends say Peggy Lee. The male: Bing Crosby. But Chuck Mancuso picks Frank. Yes, the Chairman of the Board.

2. What was your favorite pre 1960 professional football team? Most said the '49 Bills of George Ratterman, Buckets Hirsch, and Chet Mutyrn.

3. Favorite sports writer/announcer? Jim Burke and the Pub Crew anoint Phil Ranallo. Charley Bailey (Jerry Kissell's favorite) and Ralph Hubbell

garnered a few votes.

4. Favorite Honky Tonk pianist in Buffalo - Jackie Jocko – he is still playing at the Hyatt. He started at the Everglades in the 40s. He is a true Buffalo legend. Mark Russell came in second.

5. Favorite place for Beef on Weck. In 50s, Bailo's on Lovejoy. OK they got caught serving horsemeat – but that was during the war - as in "Don't you know there's a war on?"

6. Favorite Chicken Wings, - none back then. Anchor Bar did not serve them until the 60s – Before that, the wings stayed on the chicken.

7. Best Coffee shop: Deco's, a favorite for Ad Voyer and Zuke. Your Host was second. No Starbucks or Tim's in existence then.

8. Favorite downtown Christmas store window. According to Ceil Becker and Diane Faulkner, it was a tie between Hengerer's and JN Adams. Walmart had not yet taken over the world.

9. Favorite TV comedy: Mary Langenbach led the survey in choosing "I Love Lucy." For me, the Honeymooners was tops.

10. Radio comedy: The survey is incomplete but Fibber McGee and Bob Hope are running strong.

11. Best place for male college types to find summer jobs: If you lived in South Buffalo/Lackawanna it was THE steel plant. For the Northern burbs it was Continental Can. That's where Larry Cole, Big Red Delaney and Vodra (Double D) made a "killing" on the piece rate system. They relished cashing their big checks at the Colvin Gables, or was it the Treehaven?

12. Jobs for young women? Department stores, like Bergers were big. Many bobby soxers also labored as soda "jerks" at the local drug store. Back then many drug stores, had soda fountains and luncheonette areas.

13. Best big city to visit: Hands down winner: The Big Apple. NYC always was and always will be. Toronto got one vote. Our neighbor to the North is now a world class city; back then it was a sleepy little WASP

town. Buffalonians only went there for the annual CNE, Canadian National Exhibition.

14. Most popular morning news radio personality: Cline Buehlman. As in "Yours Truly Buelly."

15. Favorite cigarette: Camels or Luckies for men, Chesterfield for women. Hey! Even Joe DiMaggio smoked Cigs in the dugout.

16. Favorite DJ. Joe Rico. Top big band - Stan Kenton. Kenton even did a number for Rico, called "Jump for Joe!"

17. Favorite Sunday ride - out to Gramma's house, as in the Ol' Man barking "You kids be quiet and get in the car — we are going for a ride to ---!

18. Favorite toys: Lincoln Logs for boys. Raggedy Ann dolls for girls. How about those lead solders form World War II? Banned today — poison?

19. Favorite place to enjoy pop music? Driving around in Ace (aka Sy, Sid, Bob) Warner's 1937 ford convertible listening to the Crew Cuts belt out: Sha Sha Boom.

20. Favorite "other" store. The Army/Navy surplus store (the one next to the Town Casino was the best of several on Main Street). Remember all those neat things you could buy that the Marines used on Iwo Jima: canteens, trenching tools, pup tents, bayonets and more.

21. Favorite Buffalo Bison: For the real oldsters it was Ollie Carnegie. For others it was Luke Easter.

22. Favorite Hot Dog Stand: Pat's on Sheridan. Ted's was a distant second.

# The Senior Shuffle
Originally printed February 2016

*Walking, jogging, and running races take place every weekend of the year. Various age groups are welcome. Seniors are usually left out, but now efforts are underway to rectify that.*

The Running, Walking, Racing etc. season is about to begin.

Runners, joggers, walkers, outdoor enthusiasts, are familiar with all sorts of races. Racing in various forms has taken off these past 50 years and has become, like so many other sports, part of our national obsession. In the months ahead, there will be marathons, half marathons, quarter marathons, and mini marathons, as well as 20ks, 12ks, 10ks, 6ks, and kks. Most will benefit worthy causes: cancer cures, heart disease, kidney failures, autism, MS, AIDS, and more.

Running has been around since Homo Sapiens first stood erect; the modern obsession is a fairly recent phenomenon. My pals, Shoes and Fring recalled that, back in the 1940's, the only time we ever raced as kids was in the annual citywide track meet for grade schoolers in Delaware Park. (Of course, not counting when our friend, Zuke was running from the cops). The school principal would announce "tomorrow – tryouts for the annual track meet. Bring sneakers if you have them". Sneakers were a kind of luxury in those days; a few kids had the $3.95 Buster Browns, the rest of us had to run in our everyday shoes. We ran (practiced) for an hour and were told to return once more the following week. We ran again. Almost all qualified, although, come to think of it, there were no qualifications. We were told to show up at Delaware Park a week later and there amidst unbelievable chaos the races took place. There were many winners. In fact I think everyone was a winner because everyone received a small cloth emblem from the AAU indicating a superior athletic accomplishment. The AAU badge was promptly stashed in the top drawer of your bedroom dresser, there to remain forever.

Racing picked up momentum in the 1960's, and not just by those running to avoid the Vietnam draft. President Kennedy and his rotund press secretary, Pierre Salinger publicized physical fitness. Pretty soon half of Buffalo was jogging around Delaware Park.

In the 70's, Jim Fixx did much to popularize running with his publication, "The Complete Book of Running." Unfortunately for Ol' Jim, he ran so much that he dropped dead of a heart attack on a lonely Vermont road at age of 52, in 1984. But racing and jogging had taken off bigtime.

The local racing season, unofficially, begins early in March with the Old First Ward Shamrock Run. Bill Maloney, and Perennial Cross Country Champion (won it the year that I participated). I did finish it (an hour behind Maloney). The year's finale is the ancient and ever popular Thanksgiving Day Turkey Trot. A true Legendary Buffalo event.

In between the First Ward and the Turkey Trot, there are countless other races. In the past many were organized by the top three area racing clubs: Checkers AC, The Belle Watling Club and the Buffalo Philharmonic Club. Racing impresarios such as Carl Roesch, Bob Ivory, Jim Roberts, Jim Nowicki personified the craze as they helped to organize and officiate races. Participants come in all shapes and sizes. Some will wear the latest in expensive running gear, $400 running shoes, and flashy material to cover as little of the flesh as permissible. Some outfits are just plain goofy.

Ah, but there is still room for one more race, one just for seniors. It is about to happen. It is being discussed and organized over coffee, almost daily at the Café Aroma at Elmwood and Bidwell. Warren Crouse has appointed himself Co-Director along with Dave Costello. Celebrated Baristas: Heather, Michaela, and Justin will be honorary chairpersons of the event.

To qualify you must be on social security. Otherwise in the spirit of diversity, all are eligible. Kenyans and Ethiopians are welcome but they must be at least 62. Age discrimination does prevail. Costello, Cruse, J. Schweigel, Bill Russell, Chuck Mancuso, several Mikes, have all offered suggestions for the event's name. Senior Shuffle is popular; trending are the Geezer Grind, the Geezer Gallop and The Curmudgeon Crawl.

The race will take place on Grandparents day. It will begin at 6 AM (no problem for the oldsters). The length of the race will vary. The finish line will be at Elmwood and Bidwell. The starting line will be staggered. Those in the best shape, as determined by Charles Yeager and his Cherry Hill medical staff will start at the Café Aroma. This first group will include legitimate shufflers. Those needing a cane or walking stick will start at the Buffalo Sem; those with walkers at Soldiers Circle.

All the niceties of the traditional races will be provided. Cups of water, snifters of brandy, and bottles of Geritol, will be handed out every few yards. There will be mandatory rest stops, e.g. a short nap will be taken at the Soldiers

Place mound of dirt.

Sponsors lined up include Independent Health, Blue Cross, and AARP. Prizes will include: Hoverboard walkers with flashing lights, a two month stay in the Brothers of Mercy Nursing Home, and a tryout with the Buffalo Bills. The first prize will be a Methuselah costume, the winner then being named the official Grand Marshall for the annual Elmwood Village parade in mid-summer.

First responders will be present at appropriate intervals. Funeral directors, Roberts, Harkens, Dengler, will be present discreetly.

## Grandpa's Days - Grandpa did NOT Walk 12 Miles to School!
Originally printed February 2017

*Grandparents remember the days of the telephone party lines, of feeding coal into the hamper each winter evening, and cranking up old automobiles as well as the very first days of television. Drinking beer at 18 was also part of the era.*

At a recent basketball game with my grandsons, Nick and Joey, I noticed that both were on their cell phones while presumably also watching the game. Seemed like everyone under 35 was involved with some sort of handheld communication device!

Later, on the way home, I had a good discussion with Nick (16) and Joey (17) about all sorts of things, prompted by the universal use of cell phones. In fact our talk evolved into a look at how the present day differed from when I was their age, circa 1950, and, to add a little additional context, I noted, inter alia, how things were also so vastly different when my own grandfather was their age (circa 1900).

Here is how the session unfolded.

I said in my day we had rotary telephones, one per home. Immediately Joey said, "You mean that thing (phone) the Munschauers had in their cottage and no one knew what it was or how to us it?" I said yes, and then I explained how our phone line was shared by three other neighbors, a party line. I recall my dad occasionally complaining that that old biddy, Mabel Klutz, was hogging the line again. Nick said, "So you had no privacy?" Right, for personal calls my pals and I would hike up to Kay's drug store and use the telephone booth: 5 cents for a three minute private call to your girlfriend. I told Nick that it was kind of like he and his friends meeting at Panera's.

As for my grandfather - he had to take a horse into town to the general store and have Mr. Nosbisch ring up the number. Everyone nearby could listen in. More or less like when old Alex Bell invented the first phone just a few years earlier. Nick was astonished; indicating that he could talk in private to a person virtually anywhere on earth (in space too?).

The discussion turned to cars. Both grandsons had recently learned to drive. I noted that today's autos were splendid creations: Heated up or cooled in minutes, front wheel drive meant you could cope with all kinds of weather, and you could choose from hundreds of models in 45 colors, some of which never even existed in my day.

In the late 40s, choices were pretty much limited to Chevys and Fords. However my first was an exception; it was a '37 LaSalle, but unlike Archie Bunker's, mine did not run great. Cars often broke down, flat tires were commonplace, radiators boiled over in the summer, engine blocks cracked in the winter. Car bodies rusted out from the salt making a Buffalo owned auto easily identified.

Of course, my grandfather had to rely on horses until Henry Ford developed the Model T, or Tin Lizzie. Ol' Nellie was then put out to pasture and Gramps puttered to town with a crank handy. Nick said, "crank?" I replied that if the engine failed to start you jammed the crank under the radiator and turned it or cranked the engine a few times and the car magically started again (sometimes).

Our discussion moved on. As we motored along, I mentioned that we just had a new furnace installed. They looked quizzically as if to say "What's so big about that?" That opened the opportunity for me to return again to the 40s, proclaiming that our furnace then used coal and had a stoker. Coal? Stoker? They were again in foreign territory. I informed them how Mr. Bork, our coal man, would deliver a load of coal every few weeks. He would back up the dump truck connect a slide to the shoot that opened into the coal bin in the cellar. My task each evening was to shovel the coal into the stoker (large hamper). The filled stoker would allow coal to empty into the furnace throughout the cold night hours keeping the house warm. Then the tough part: lugging out the cans of ashes. Hauling ashes was heavy work.

Our conversation turned to television. Now there was another huge contrast. Joey said he could watch hundreds of programs on TV, computer, internet, on demand, and so forth and tape or delay them for any time of day.

He could watch reruns of "the Office" or "Dead Man Walking" whenever he wished.

But in the 40s, we were part of the golden age of radio, The Lone Ranger, Bob Hope, Fibber McGee, Captain Midnight, and The Shadow. Television made its appearance in Buffalo in 1948. We saw it first in the windows of local appliance stores. People would gather about 4 pm, that's when programming started. First we saw the test pattern, itself a thing of wonder! Then came Kukla, Fran, and Ollie, a little later the Milton Berle show. "Uncle Miltie" was the first big TV star. Following that you caught the harness racers from Yonkers raceway. It was that or nothing. Then you went home.

Then came 1951 and millions of middle class Americans purchased TV sets. The Television Age had arrived. Nicely, it coincided with the advent of the drinking age for us.

The segue here is that saloons/taverns were among the first places to have television sets. Yes, sitting betwixt the bottles of Three Feathers and Seagrams on the back bar would be a 12 inch black and white Admiral guaranteed to begin the downward plunge of your good eyesight. But you could catch sports, especially boxing and at least six nights a week.

Joey's interest perked up. "You guys drank at 18?" I responded "Yeah, but beer primarily and no binge drinking." "Craft beer?" said Nick. I replied: "never heard of it." Our favorites were usually Jenny or Iroquois. A little later Carlings Black Label made a big splash.

Then I disclosed a big secret. No credit cards existed, but you could run a bar tab. You just said to Jack Keegan, proprietor of the Kenmore Tavern: "put it on my tab, Jack." Now that was really coming of age - when the bar owner allowed you to "run" a tab. Your pronouncement indicated a true person of importance! And you said it loud enough so the unfortunate customers without a tab could hear. Nick seemed impressed, not sure about Joey; as for me I just beamed.

Ah, what great memories!

We arrived home! I left the grandkids with this one myth-buster: "No. I did NOT walk 12 miles to school."

*Tuesday night stalwarts at the Wellington Pub. Left to right: Reister, Dickerson, Christiano, McNicholas, McElroy, Burke (fearless leader)*

*Kenmore geezers at the River Grill, Left to right: Zimmer, G. Warner, Sid Warner, Ad Voyer, Lee R., Starr, Fring in foreground*

*Kenmore H.S. 1952 reunion: Larry Cole, Tony Evans and Cliff (the Brow) Lang*

*St Paul's class of '48, Left to right: Dr. Faulkner, B. Dietrich, P. Young, J. Duggan, B. Smith, B. Farrington, M. Langenback*

*Larry Cole, Tony Evans and Sid Warner near the Kenmore Tavern*

*Frank Eberl – Popular Breakfast Master of Ceremonies*

# Labor Day – End of Summer
Originally printed September 2010

*Labor Day traditionally has meant the end of summer. It has also meant other things to Americans of all ages over the years. It is a time for picnics, celebrations, and festivals, as well as the time to prepare to get back to school and serious work.*

Everyone knows Labor Day is the first Monday in September. Not everyone knows that it began as a tribute to the laboring man in America. Today most think of it primarily as the unofficial last day of summer.

In the 19th century, when so many of our forefathers were recent immigrants who worked in the factories, mills, and mines of America, the labor movement was in its infancy. The industrial revolution was new. The laboring man was viewed as a rather sweaty, somewhat ignorant type, hardly a respected member of the community. He was poorly paid, had no benefits, and was often a victim of job-ending industrial accidents. Unfortunately the workers of the 1880s were often associated with anarchists, Bolsheviks, and other radical fringe elements. But then some cities and states, and by the early 20th century, the nation, saw fit to legislate a day honoring the working man of America. Thus Labor Day was born, a day to bestow dignity on the skilled and unskilled workers of our country. In the years that followed politicians (naturally) and union leaders gave speeches, headed parades and joined in celebrations at which the virtues of the laboring man were remembered.

As the 20th century moved along, the labor movement and the unions changed. Workers shared in America's post World War II affluence, owning a house and auto, going on vacations and sending their children to college. The economy changed from an industrial to a service oriented one. The traditional trade unions shrunk; powerful public sector unions - teachers, police and firemen –came to dominate. Basically they were well fed members of the middle class feeding in part – at the public trough (for life!).

Meanwhile the celebration of Labor Day was also changing. The laboring man, the type epitomized by Ray "the Bull" Smith, was pretty much forgotten, or put on the backburner.

Today Labor Day continues to signify that a new school year is beginning.

For many, Labor Day means boarding up the summer cottage, storing the boats, putting away the bathing suits.

For youngsters, it means good bye to camps and the new friends they met whom they swore they would keep in touch with forever.

For sports fans, Labor Day marks the beginning of the football season, which is manifestly untrue since football kicks off long before that holiday.

For the 20 somethings –Labor Day means an end of frolicking and boozing at the beach front saloons on Lake Erie. Some of life's most memorable moments occur when you are that age. Back in the 50s, for the "after 50 crowd", Labor Day meant saying goodbye to the guys and dolls at Sunset Inn, or Sneaky Pete's or Sheehan's near Crystal Beach, but especially Lerczak's! Oh there were other colorful watering holes, but Lerczak's was the icon of the generation. For the nostalgic minded, now in the 60 to 80 age range, Lerczak's continues to hold sway like the Canadiana, the Comet at Crystal Beach, The Palace Burlesk or Pat's Hot Dog Stand.

No place rivaled Lerczak's. It was THE place to be and be seen. "Ma" Lerczak herself was a legend, patrolling near the entrance, in her well-worn red woolen sweater, with her attractive daughters presiding over a host of bartenders and waitresses. "Ma" was in control. The place was always packed. Sing Alongs broke out spontaneously – often begun with "I love Paris in the Springtime." The famous log cabin drinking establishment stood between the South Shore Inn and Bill Miller's Bar (where you could rent a room for $4 including pillow and blanket – no sheets) and not risk the long ride back to Buffalo. Next door was Jimmy Goodrich's fairly classy saloon, run by the Champion boxer of the 1920s. There you were on your best behavior – otherwise you were ousted.

After a few hours of swilling down Black Labels or Genesees (Schlitz *said* *& Done* was the premium beer in those days), it was time for the traditional hot dog at Connors Stand. If you stayed overnight, your choice was your sleeping bag near the tennis courts, (you rose at the crack at dawn to avoid the local authorities) or crashing in a "new friend's" cottage. Or you might risk the drive back to Buffalo (and it was a risk if you drove in Sid Warner's 48 Chevy convertible, radio blasting the Crews Cuts Sh-Boom at 90 decibels, with Ad Voyer riding Shotgun and you sandwiched in the back with Larry Cole, the Fringer, and Shoes Bewick).

If you weren't drinking, you might have been dancing. Labor Day also meant the swan song for the dance halls in Canada at Morgan's Point, Long Beach, and the fabulous Crystal Ballroom at Crystal Beach. In its expansive ballroom featured the bands of Tommy Dorsey, Glen Miller's group under Ray McKinley, Woody Herman, and of course, the big guy Stan Kenton, with his lead singer the marvelous June Christy (The Misty Miss Christy). Joe Rico, top rated DJ "Jump for Joe" made us aware of the majesty of those bands especially the Kenton one.

In the last analysis, Labor Day – pure and simple – meant the unofficial end of summer. Period.

# Chapter 5. Those Wonderful Teen Years

*Youth, in the years following World War II, were addicted to the Lone Ranger (on radio later on TV), shoveled snow (and other odd jobs) for cash, enjoyed old fashioned Christmases, gathered on a town's main avenues, (no malls then), and patronized hot dog stands (no McDonald's then).*

## Did the Lone Ranger Drink Craft Beer???

Originally printed April 2014

*Older generations, those who grew up watching the Lone Ranger had plenty of local beers available. Today it is not uncommon for a saloon to have 15 or more craft beers on tap. Craft beer, social media, and political correctness are everywhere.*

What do craft beer, the Lone Ranger, and a 49 cent stamp have in common? Not much. So this column is about "nothing", as Seinfeld used to say. Well, no common thread, anyway. Paid columnists, e.g. Jerry Sullivan, do this occasionally. It is a nice way to comment on several subjects - about which individually you would not want to devote an entire column.

Take craft beer as an example. Has the beer industry as we know it gone to pot? (Not Colorado pot) Where did CRAFT originate? Craft - isn't that from Boy Scout camp as in arts and crafts? A while back we had microbreweries. Fine! But Craft? In the 50s we had local beer, Iroquois, Simons and some premium, like in "Hey Bartender - I just got paid – I'll splurge for a Schlitz," (or a Bud, Pabst, Blatz). NYC gave us Rheingold (the Rheingold Girl second only to Miss America) Canadian brew - you had to go to Ft. Erie for an O'Keefe's; in springtime we had bock beer.

And now we have craft: Amber, wheat, oat, white, alfalfa, all that stuff labeled as craft beer! It's a crime. I thought I had seen it all until my niece Lib came over with something called "New Planet - gluten free pale ale," made from sorghum and brown rice extract???? And no, I don't think the Chinese concocted it. Enough said "make mine Manru!"

What about the Lone Ranger! Talk about wonderful childhood memories? Turn on the radio on Tuesday night and listen up: "Out of the past … the hoof beats of the great horse Silver" and "Who was that Masked Man?" and "Hi ho Silver, away." Good stuff and a terrific program! The Indian Tonto was not servile; he was the white guy's "faithful companion." Tonto had dignity; one might even make a case for him as an environmental pioneer, promoting the best interests of the Great West.

So a few years ago, in our politically correct age, a new film comes out on the Lone Ranger. Johnny Depp "stars" as Tonto but actually Tonto is called the "native American Spirit Warrior Tonto."

How's that for a moniker? Depp looked goofy. The film received negative reviews and was a commercial failure. Having taught American history for decades, I agree that the American Indian was treated horribly. But in this case, Tonto was the Lone Ranger's "faithful Indian companion," in turn the Lone Ranger was Tonto's trusted friend, Kemo Sabe. Tonto – in yesteryear was played by Jay Silverheels, of the Mohawk tribe in Ontario. Not sure of the inept Depp's genealogy!

This issue brings back memories of the old Shea's North Park theater – on Hertel Ave., recently gentrified into a splendid showplace. I hope that co-owner Mike Christiano shows some of those old serials or shorts from yesteryear: like Don Winslow and the Coast Guard, the Adventures of Captain Marvel, the Green Hornet, and Professor Dave Cos's favorite, the purple Monster Strikes. And of course the Lone Ranger! We can count on Dr. Ray Barker, the North Park's all around film expert, to offer some of the best.

How about Michael Sam! Okay - big news when the All American football player from Missouri came out – as gay. But the media carried the news to the extreme. After querying my friends, both on the left and right, and also gay and non-gay, there was unanimity as in "so what! He's gay. Let it rest." Sam had been a great college football player and he may be a standout in the NFL. Incidentally, this story was not in the same ball park as the Jackie Robinson story.

In fact Michael Sam is already old news – the mercurial public has already forgotten about Sam and moved on to the next NFL issue.

Ban the N word! Penalize a team 15 yards if its player uses it! Is this political correctness gone absurd? Besides I understand that the N word is mostly used by black rappers? Everyone I know agrees that the N word has no place in American life. But a football penalty! What about the F word. If that were banned no one would be left playing on the gridiron. What about the G word – Gay! And how about taking God's name in vain! Did not Moses have some laws forbidding that?

A few other items – which can rankle and try one's sanity?

First class mail - raised a few cents to 49 Cents. Come on now, why not 50 cents. It might even help bail out the Postal Service. But 49 cents! Can you picture yourself asking for a first class stamp, giving the clerk 50 cents, she's out of pennies and has to go to the backroom to get a roll? So you are standing there, with a few grumbling grumps behind you, waiting for your penny change. On the other hand Canada raised its first class mail to $1.00. Does Canada need the extra revenue for the rehabilitation of Justin Bieber and Toronto's Mayor, Rob Ford?

*Lone Ranger and Tonto: Extremely
popular on radio then on TV*

# Before McDonalds there was Pat's Hot Dog Stand
Originally printed September 2011

*There were many popular meeting places for teenagers in the 1950s, but none were as famous as Pat's. Pat's Hot Dog Stand on Sheridan Drive was a mecca; it drew people from all over the region who often stood in long lines waiting for a charcoal broiled dog.*

Ray Kroc opened his first McDonalds in San Bernardino, California in 1955 and the rest is – as they say- history. McDonalds, along with Burger King, Wendy's and KFC grew steadily in the 1960s and eventually covered the entire universe.

Teenagers find it incredible but there was actually a time when none of those fast food places existed. Where did teenagers go, where did anyone go who wanted a snack, "fast food?" Actually 60 years ago there were many favorite food spots, places to "hang out" or, in today's lingo, just "hang," most individually owned and operated.

I was reminded of this recently when Prof. Bob Butler noted that a bank at Sheridan and Colvin was uncovering a sign that indicated that once Brinsons stood there. Yes Brinson's hotdog stand stood at that busy intersection from the 1930s to 1960s. Recently Paul Brinson passed away; he had worked at his father's, the original. Later he opened his own hot dog stand at Sheridan and Military, but the original Brinson was the place to be for the youth of Tonawanda, North Buffalo, Kenmore, and beyond. At least for a time, that is, until the legendary Pat's hit the scene. (Later to be replaced by Ted's).

Ted's, now synonymous with Sahlen's charcoaled dogs, throughout WNY, started with Ted himself on a horse drawn cart pedaling his wares. By the 40s, Ted was operating out of a shed at the base of the Peace Bridge amidst swarms of sand flies. (Unlike the seagulls at the Hatch, they ate little but annoyed much). Later Ted's opened in Tonawanda. As Buffalonians migrated to the rest of the U.S., the name and fame of Ted's as well as Sahlen's, accompanied them.

Back then, Sahlen's was just one of several good brands of hot dogs. Malecki and Wardynski were more popular, and the number 1 brand, by far, was Szalogowski. "Shellys" were the best.

Circa 1950, the corner drug store was always a favorite gathering place, all neighborhoods had one. That was also true of ice cream parlors, and luncheonettes with counter service. Deco's seemed ubiquitous, the Tim Horton's of the period. Begun in 1917-1918 by Greg Deck, the chain eventually covered Buffalo with some 37 outlets advertising Buffalo's Best cup of coffee. After WWII, Your Host emerged to offer some competition. The Host started as a hot dog stand, located on Kenmore Avenue near the Englewood railroad line, with Jack "Arnie" Arnet at the helm.

And there were others. In South Buffalo, teens congregated at Sullivans, which Bill Carey claims was a stepping stone to Cooley's saloon. Percy's and Unterreicher's on Hertel were favorites with the North Buffalo crowd, as was the legendary Cardina's on Parkside – frequented by the likes of Jim Burke and Wayne Reilly in their pre-Park Meadow days. The Alcobar in Kenmore hosted swarms of teenagers. Ja Fa Fa's in Cheektowaga did likewise. WNY Historian Joe Beiron claims that there was a popular hot dog stand near the Crossroads Restaurant on Harlem (famous for swallowing a gold fish in your beer). Ye Gads, I still think I have one swimming in my stomach. Connors, across from Lerczak's, was another dog stand of renown. In Central Buffalo, the Town House and Decos were the places to go, according to George Dixon and John Christiano. Leroy Chollet's (Canisius Basketball Legend) hot dog stand on Delavan near Main was a hit, briefly.

Out in the growing suburbs, Amherst, Tonawanda, and Kenmore there were a number of attractive spots. Mike Parco, one of Buffalo's premier golfers in the late 40s opened a driving range on Delaware just north of Elmlawn cemetery (near the site of WWII victory gardens) and with it a hot dog stand. Foster Brooks, later nationally celebrated comedian, teamed up with hockey star, Freddie Hunt (whose illustrious career took him right into Sabre management in the 70s) to open a hot dog stand at the corner of Sheridan and Delaware. Brooks and Hunt were much more successful in other occupations as was Parco.

I am sure After 50 readers can think of others. But for Western New Yorkers, now in the 70-80 age cohort, nothing surpassed Pat's.

Pat's was the place to be seen. On a summer evening guys would sputter up to Pat's in their jalopies; others would screech up in "hot rods", pick up a few dogs and burn rubber as they sped off. Still others would pull up in a '41 Plymouth with rumble seat – any set of wheels that might attract that cute blond.

What was distinctive about Pats was the seemingly endless hot dog line formed in front of the charcoal grills; it resembled the assembly line at the Chevy plant. You ordered a drink, fries, and then the dogs. Several guys worked the grill, veritable icons in their own mind, as in "Hey, I have a job grilling dogs at Pat's."

The charcoal grillers achieved status, kind of like famous bartenders, Tom Harkens at the Circle of Thieves or Kevin Godzich at Adam's Rib. They were persons of esteem, they had made it, there was nothing else left to do in life in the 50's other than follow Jack Kerouac out west (as Sonny and Klu did).

Pat's is gone (replaced by, what else, a Walgreens). The Golden Arches are everywhere. Fortunately Ted's survives and thrives.

*Pat's Hot Dogs - Sheridan Drive*

# Delaware Avenue in Kenmore - The "Main Drag"

Originally printed May 2011

*If you lived in Kenmore/Tonawanda in the 1940-1970 Era, Delaware Avenue from Kenmore Avenue to Sheridan Drive is where the action was. Eating, drinking, shopping, banking, it was all there.*

Buffalo and suburbs – vibrant neighborhoods - each with a main avenue - was where all the action was. Main St. in Williamsville, Seneca in South Buffalo, Grant on the West Side, Broadway in East Buffalo, Hertel in North Buffalo and more. "After 50" readers can relate to these.

For me it was Delaware Ave in Kenmore. Kenmore had Military Road, with a grimy assortment of saloons quenching the thirst of nearby factories workers, Elmwood had a few stores, Colvin simply had houses, and Kenmore Avenue had potholes and Dates Laundry. But Delaware Avenue – that was the main scene. But how it has changed? Only a few iconic edifices remain from the 1940s.

One of those – the Wheelchair home (Originally Eberhardt's homestead) sits at the corner of Delaware and Kenmore Avenue. Halfway through the village stands the municipal building. Not much else is left. True - some commercial structures remain from that era but the occupants we knew from 6 decades ago are long gone.

So you - the "After 50" generation - follow the yellow brick road, circa 1949, North on Delaware. Opposite the wheelchair home was Loves candy store, Klipples bar ( you had to be at least 15 to be served a Jenny), The Kenmore News shop, (phones to place your horse bets) and Tremos' greasy spoon featuring Texas red hots.

Nearby was the YWCA. Its first floor pool tables often witnessed the fabled Duffys "run the table." A few blocks away between Parkwood and Euclid was Crane's bar, a favorite watering hole for the geezer set. The Christian Science reading room, diligently avoided by the patrons of Cranes, was at the corner. A block away was Al Caruso's shoe shop, near the famous Trabert's family restaurant. Lee Trabert recalls that the business could not survive the Black Market of the war years so it vanished.

Delaware Avenue was home to a number of independently owned pharmacies. Owners were almost always present in this pre-Walgreen era. Some had lunch counters, ideal meeting places to have an ice cream sundae. Donovans, Parsons, and the North End pharmacy were such oases of pleasure. Kays was probably the most famous drug store, mainly because of its central location at Lincoln and Delaware. At the very front was a busy tobacco counter; Luckys or Camels for 15 cents a pack (now about 15 dollars?) - as a right of passage you had to be at least 13 before you started to smoke; also the phone booth was popular – teenage boys could dial up their girlfriends and mutter sweet nothings – until told to leave since important neighbors like Jim Banigan or the Langenbachs might need to use the phone.

The most popular "hangout" for teens was the Alcobar. It remained so for decades. Students from St. Joes, the "Mount", Kenmore High, and Canisius met about 3 in the afternoon, dime in hand to buy a chocolate phosphate, and spend an hour gabbing. Should someone become rowdy, Big Lou Watson, co-owner, would escort (or toss) the perpetrator out – admonishing him not to return until properly repentant.

There were several grocery stores. Some like Crispells and Drennans were called delicatessens - probably because they had a meat counter. Others were forerunners of today's giants, Tops and Wegmans. Near Warren was a Nu-Way, near Girard, an A & P. And a real oldie, the Mohican Market (sawdust on the floor and barrels of pickles) was across from the all night Deco's (remember Buffalo's best cup of coffee - over 37 locations). Next door was Henel's dairy, its little diary trucks delivered milk – in glass bottles – house to house, youngsters would be given a chip of ice on hot summer days.

And then there was "Ol' Man" Moore's produce stand. He was the father of the Lieutenant Governor of New York, but that did not deter my pal, Bedwick, from taunting him, to the extent that Ol' Man Moore fired a large potato at Bedwick, clipping him on the behind and causing a loud yelp heard for miles or so legend has it.

The avenue also was home to Western Auto, Noah's Ark, and three 5 & 10 cent stores, Kresges, Woolworths, and Grants – kind of like the Dollar Generals of today. There were a number of clothing establishments, including one run by the famous five Sweeney brothers. All five served in WWII. Also jewelry stores (Moeloth and Hofert), shoe stores (Seiferts, Kenmore Boot Shop), banks, and a Gulf station run by the Grimmer boys. Nash road was a beehive of activity what with Kenmore Motors on the corner and the fire and police stations and post office in the same block. A couple of old time diners (railroad car types) near Nash and near Kinsey were vintage sites.

And the icons of all icons, the Kenmore Tavern and Golden Pheasant (to locals - the KT and The Bird).

The KT also served as a kind of recruiting station. There Marty Grant, Pete Warnock, Walt Sweeney, Zuke Morris, and yours truly, decided that it was time to join the army and off we went – from the famous KT porch - to the downtown post office to serve our country (and get the GI Bill).

Later Sonny Stuch and Zuke "resided," rather slept there; I think Dick Bing did too – in the Spartan second floor rooms, complete with bed, chair and lamp. Jack Kegan ran the joint, once he introduced hot dogs broiled in a small rotisserie; they were barely edible. Of course after a night of swilling down many Carlings, they seemed like filet mignon.

The Golden Pheasant was almost as legendary. Joe Stepanic ran it, later Mayor Wally Boehm did. It had a magnificent large oval bar and a crummy men's room. Once someone warned that the State Liquor Authority required that food be served; a small grill was purchased; grilled cheese on rye was available (occasionally).

The Kenmore theater block was the village's nerve center. In pre-television days, the movie theater - Shea's Kenmore – was the place to be. My pals and I were frequently non-paying patrons, we rapped at the fire escape door and Red the janitor would open it, but if Red was off, then one of us would pay the admission and at the appointed moment open the fire exit; 5 of us who rush in and scatter to the far recesses, while Jimmy, the usher, outfitted in short blue jacket with flashlight in hand would catch one of us. The unlucky captive would be evicted; the rest enjoyed the films.

And there was much more: bowling alleys, barber shops, stores of every variety. Space is limited, maybe another column later. Thanks to town historian John Percy and village historian Ed Adamzcak, Kenmore's memories are permanent preserved.

*The Iconic Kenmore Tavern: The most famous watering hole in the village*

*Kay's Drug Store at Delaware and Lincoln*

# Hooray for the First Snowstorm
Originally printed January 2017

*Seventy years ago the first snowstorm of the season meant a chance to make money shoveling neighbors' driveways. Following that, it was time for fun: sledding, hitching on cars, and more.*

Hooray the snow has arrived. 70 years ago that was an exciting refrain for me, my friends and many red blooded 12-13 year olds. The first snowfall of the season meant a number of things. First it meant you could make a few extra dollars shoveling neighbors' walks and driveways. You could buy your Mom a Christmas gift and have a little change for spending with your pals at the Alcobar. Secondly the welcome snow meant all kinds of outdoor activities not available since the previous winter.

Seventy years ago there were only a few ways a kid could make a few bucks; that is, in the years before he or she was eligible for working papers. A 12 or 13 year old could deliver the News or Courier or some magazines like Colliers and the Saturday Evening Post or, in the summer, caddy or mow lawns. Wintertime meant shoveling snow.

Once the snow arrived, I announced to the family that I would be headed out to shovel. Mom would then say, "Bundle up." "Where is your cap, your gloves?" "Put on your boots (arctics), even with a broken buckle or two." All kids' arctics had broken buckles. Finally she added: "Make sure you put on a scarf before you leave this house."

Once I passed inspection it was off to the garage to pick up the snow shovel. Not a light fiber glass one like today, but a shovel of heavy metal to which the snow often stubbornly clung. Snow shoveling was not a pleasant job.

I headed down the street to Mr. Hinkson's house. He had a long driveway so he was good for at least $2.00. Next was ol' man Brooks; as long as I got there before my competition, Gus Holmberg or a kid, named Herbie. Brooks was good for at least a buck but the drawback was that he always wanted to talk. I mean - Didn't he know that I was a businessman on the make? With no time for small talk! I was a working stiff; on to the next customer.

Next on my list was Mr. Warner. Sid Warner was reliable but he was also known as the neighborhood cheapskate. He always said he would give you a buck. But when finished shoveling, Mr. Warner would meet you at the door and give you 90 cents saying that was all he had then, but would give you a dime later. Which he never did! There was a story that circulated that when Sid Warner was young, he collected gas money from all his friends who wanted a ride. He collected much more than he spent on gas. When questioned - Sid said the balance was for wear and tear on his car.

Once the money making business of shoveling was finished, you hung up the shovel to await the next storm. It was now time for fun in the white stuff.

Fun meant snowball fights. Pepper the girls; once they ran away to make snow angels, we would turn our attention to other guys (the enemy) and have a free for all. On the weekends we might hike to Delaware Park, to the hill near Nottingham for sledding or skiing. Sleds had steel blades, often dangerous. Skis were wooden slats with bands to wrap around your feet, a far cry from the expensive equipment used by the Lindsey Vonn "wanna-bes" at Holiday Valley today, or even a venerable Dick Munschauer. Occasionally it was off to Sheridan Park or even Chestnut Ridge for tobogganing. Or for Illos, Longo and cohorts it was off to LaSalle or Front Park.

In the early evening, the real fun began: hitching rides on the bumpers on the back of cars. I checked on google and "snow-skitching" is the term sometimes used today. Parents warned against it, but the warnings went unheeded. It was too much fun. Yes, there was danger, but I only recall scrapes and bruises and a little blood now and then, that would happen when the car ran over some dry pavement. Usually the worst was that you ruined your boots and put a big hole in your corduroy knickers. Here is how it worked; you and your pals, e.g. Grimmer, Duggan, Bork, would hide behind neighbors' hedges, waiting for a car to stop at the corner. The car stops, you crouch down and run behind the car grabbing the bumper (bumpers were easy to grab in those days) and off you went. You hung on for 40 or 50 yards or just before the car stopped again. Then you fled the scene.

Hockey! What was that? Something the Bisons played in the AUD and a few wealthy kids played at Nichols. Oh there were a few futile attempts at playing hockey in a flooded backyard or on an icy street. But they came to naught. I do not recall a Gil Perrault coming off the streets of Buffalo heading to the NHL. Oh, I know there was an arena in Fort Erie. Still hockey was for a distinct minority.

Today of course ice rinks abound in our area. You can find kids about 22 inches tall, "skating" up and down a rink in full battle gear (or 70 pounds of

NHL hockey equipment). Meanwhile their parents ready themselves to spend almost all winter weekends bussing them throughout the Northeast. Part of a hockey travel team or entourage! Is that fun or cruel and unusual punishment?

Today too thousands of people of all ages flock to the ski slopes south of Buffalo. The moneyed class takes off for Colorado, British Columbia and Switzerland. Hockey enthusiasts blanket the metro area. And in the rejuvenated downtown Buffalo, all Western New Yorkers have unprecedented winter opportunities at Canal Side and Harbor Place. Just amazing! Who would have though it: 70 years ago or 40 years ago or even 20 years ago?

## Jeans for Christmas
Originally printed January 2011

*At one time jeans had a fairly limited market. Basically they were work clothes. Now they come in all shapes and fashions, varying in price from cheap to priceless and are worn for nearly any conceivable occasion.*

What did you get for Christmas? One of the most often heard seasonal questions ever. Or – slight variation – was Santa good to you?

Little boys, teenagers, males in general, seem to prefer sports items. Since the birth of Title IX that goes for young women too. Warm up outfits, hockey skates, ski equipment, and thousands of other jock items are all coveted. No surprise there. The shopping malls are full of sports items. What amazed me, however, on one of my seldom mall ventures, was the omnipresence of jeans.

Yes jeans! Blue jeans. I am convinced that people of all shapes and ages must receive jeans as gifts. Not only were the stores selling a vast variety of jeans, but 90% of the guys, (fewer of the females) of whatever age, seemed to be wearing jeans. Jeans are everywhere. And therefore many jeans must be given as Christmas presents.

There are jeans that sell for hundreds of dollars (no doubt a thousand at Nieman Marcus); and there are jeans that you can pick up inexpensively. Some look classy and some look as though they were retrieved from the local garbage dump. There are designer jeans. Gloria Vanderbilt even has a line. There are classic jeans, Pull on jeans, denim legging jeans, power stretched, and more.

I observed some horribly overweight people wearing, or almost wearing, jeans. They looked comical. Some very slim women wore them – they looked better; they seemed to have been poured into their jeans (perhaps they were just painted on their legs). I mean: How do they get into those? Remember Brooks Sheilds and her sexy Calvin Klein jeans?

Sometimes you see the guys with jeans kind of clinging for dear life below their backsides, as though they had to get dressed in a hurry because their house was on fire or perhaps their underpants were ablaze. Some say it is fashionable to have jeans falling down so that you can display your underwear.

Some guys wear jeans that are dirty, soiled, greasy, and give off an odor reminiscent of a pig sty. I'll bet that a respectable pig would not be caught dead in them. Others insist on wearing jeans with gaping holes or rips in them. I am told that you can purchase jeans with appropriate rips so you don't have to do the ripping yourself. That's considered "cool."

Jeans make the world go round. They are ubiquitous. But it was not always so. When I was young, we wore corduroy knickers to school. That was many decades ago. We then graduated to long pants, and those included denim jeans. (My generation preferred Khakis; we often referred to them as suntans.) Fringer was as exception – his mother insisted he wear knickers until he was a teenager.

Jeans have been around for generations. In fact Levi Strauss is credited with patenting them in 1873. Over the years, other words have been used, kind of interchangeably – like dungarees or Levis or Lees or even Wranglers. Or Overalls, though that label was pretty much reserved for the bibbed type with over the shoulder straps with plenty of pockets and hooks to hang things on. But jeans were worn sparingly back 60 years ago. They were for kids to play in, for blue collar workers to work in, and for farm folk to farm in.

The baby boomer generation changed all that. Since the 1960s jeans have become the uniform of the day for just about everyone. Jeans are everywhere. On airplanes, where people used to dress up, now jeans are as necessary for getting on board as a body search. In downtown businesses you find guys in coat and tie, and jeans. I bet that young billionaire Facebook inventor, Mike Zuckerberg, has never been out of jeans.

I have noticed jeans are not prevalent among the over 70 age group. There are a few people whom I just could not envision in a pair of jeans. My good friend, Elmira Dave, might wear tattered old slacks while digging up the flower beds for Ann, but no jeans.

# Christmas – Decades Ago
Originally printed December 2011

*Christmas has always been a wonderful time of the year. Decades ago downtown Buffalo was the destination for all kids. Very similar to the TV classic: The Christmas Story by Jean Shepherd.*

Christmas – 60 – 70 years ago. The good old days! Yes – in some ways and No - not if one expected lots of presents.

A toy – just one - plus mittens and a woolen cap. That's about all that a child (circa. 1940) might expect. Lincoln logs, tinker toys, erector sets for boys, Raggedy Ann dolls, paper dolls or even storybook dolls, for girls. Those were the hot items. Comic books too. My pal, Jack Duggan always got comic books to add to his massive collection. Captain Marvel was his favorite. Money was scarce during the Depression. Despite the return of prosperity during WWII, there continued to be a severe shortage of consumer goods in the 1940s. Howitzers and fighter planes were being produced in abundance, real weapons for use on the battlefields of Europe and the islands of the Pacific.

The big question for little kids back then: where was the "real" Santa? Various neighborhood business streets had a Salvation Army Santa. He might be a seaman off a lake freighter frozen for the winter in the Port of Buffalo. Other times he might be a barfly from the House of Quinn in need of a few bucks for his daily bottle of Gallo. These grimy bearded Santas wore ill-fitting Santa Claus outfits, and goofy looking, soiled caps. They tried to keep warm by ringing bells or playing havoc on a tarnished horn of some sort.

Children all knew that the real Santa was in one of the large downtown department stores. Was it Hengerers or JN Adams? Santa just had to be in one or the other because those stores had the colorful display windows featuring the latest toys, especially toys with moving parts. The Lionel electric train layouts were a marvel to behold. Nearby would be a manger scene – those were not outlawed yet. My brother and I would hurry into the department store, up the escalator to the top floor, and there was the big guy - resplendent with white beard, brilliant red suit, and a belly that shook "like a bowlful of jelly." Boy! Were we ever on our best behavior! A reward: Mom took us to lunch at either Laube's Old Spain or MacDoel's.

Live Christmas trees were a must. Often they were purchased at the last minute on Christmas Eve, possibly from Clyde Corwall in his lot across from Shea's Kenmore Theater. You might end up with a pitiful tree with a gaping hole. Mom to the rescue – she covered that hole with a bunch of icicles. Back in 1939, we actually saw Santa bring a tree to our house. Santa, I found out later, was Uncle Red. Never saw him again, he left for the Navy - his ship was sunk in the Atlantic at the beginning of WWII. Trees stayed up until at least White Christmas – that's when the Russians celebrated (the good Russkies, not those "commies"). Today trees are put up shortly after Thanksgiving, and packed away (since most are now artificial) on December 26.

Want a wonderful picture of what Christmas was like long ago? Watch the classic film, A Christmas Story, by Jean Shepherd. I never tire of watching it, perhaps because I knew "Shep," well I sort of knew him. In the 50s Jean Shepherd had a nightly radio program on WOR in NYC. He just talked and talked, an unrivalled raconteur. His masterpiece film is set in his hometown near Gary, Indiana (a steel town not unlike Buffalo).

Christmas dinner was a major event. The smells that wafted from Mom's kitchen were virtually sensuous. Christmas dinner meant the entire family crowded around the dining room table with a few card tables for the overflow. Even grandma was there - having not yet been relegated to some forlorn old folks home.

Church too, was a priority. Midnight Mass for Catholics (Fr. Ring always asked for a green Christmas). The best of Christmas music (Handel's "Messiah") sung by choirs at Westminster Presbyterian or St. Paul's Episcopal. What was Christmas without honoring Christ?! Today, the politically correct types are content to utter: "Happy Holidays." Too bad!

Over the decades, Christmas has changed in many ways, tree lights are much better. Remember those old strings of lights? If one went out, then you had to spend hours testing each one separately as Elaine Navaugh used to do in the Humboldt Park neighborhood.

Kids now have more toys than in the past. Drive by a driveway sale and notice the piles of Fisher Price or Mattel toys. Surely an indication that children now get so much STUFF that they do not have time to use all if it, much less break it.

Christmas dinner is still a warm wonderful event with much of the family present. Unfortunately there are now so many fragmented families, you are not always sure if you're sitting next to a child of the first or third marriage of

Brother Bill or the second wife of Cousin Jake, or just his significant other.

Many people still attend Christmas religious services. Now it might be a mega church (Joel Osteen's amphitheater in Houston) or it might be Pastor Pat's much smaller edifice, the Church of the Nazarene in Amherst. Splendid Cathedrals continue to draw flocks of the faithful.

Christmas continues to be, in the words of the popular song, "the most wonderful time of the year." People are quite generous during the Christmas season. Food and toy collections abound. Lots of people do lots of wonderful things for the needy. Yes Virginia, there is a Santa.

# Chapter 6. College Basketball – AUD

There was a time, approximately from the 1940s into the 1960s, when college basketball was huge in Buffalo. National sports authorities said that Buffalo's Memorial Auditorium (the AUD) was second only to Madison Square Garden, as a popular mecca for the sport.

## Basketball – the Way it Was – 50 Years Ago
Originally printed December 2010

*For the after 70 (?) guys, basketball was THE wintertime sport. It was virtually universal; just a handful of guys played hockey then. A few went skiing. Most played basketball. Basketball in the 50s was simple: put on your inexpensive sneakers, grab a ball, find a gym, round up a few guys, choose sides, and go at it.*

A few generations ago, basketball stood alone as THE activity for winter (which, by the way, is why James Naismith invented it). A future column will focus on the outstanding college varsity quintets in the 1940-60 era. But now the real amateurs deserve some attention. Virtually every youth seemed to played basketball in those days. Skiing was something done at Lake Placid, in fact the only experience most youngsters had with skiing was to slip into a couple of wooden slats and tumble down the "towering" slopes in Delaware Park. As for hockey, the best site that an ordinary youth could find was a frozen tennis court often with more potholes than Kenmore Avenue in February. Today, and since the arrival of the Sabres 40 years ago, amateur hockey seems ubiquitous.

In the good ol' days (don't you love that phrase?) it was either basketball or stay inside and play monopoly. Almost every school had a gym of varying degrees of playability. Cracked floorboards, low hanging lights- an electrical hazard, steel girders blocking a shot at the basket, and overhanging balconies were not uncommon. That was part of the game. Access to a local gym was easy if you were involved with some sort of organized team, otherwise you were on your own. If you knew the janitor (custodian or sanitary engineer), you might get him to let you in. The other option was to find an unlocked window; you then played until discovered and evicted. That is the way it went.

In those days, there were many basketball "wannabes," guys who played at various levels, guys who "almost made the varsity." One was Bob Farrington, a deft lefty from St. Bona. Bob developed a virtually unstoppable hook shot, deadly from inside the perimeter (where was that perimeter, anyway?). He was lean and rangy; he practiced with the likes of Tom Stith, in the Olean Armory, often at the expense of his philosophy class. Bob was always hopeful of making the varsity - but he didn't. He played for the KT (Kenmore Tavern) Turtles where he teamed with John "Shoes" Bewick, a bulky 6 foot plus center who scored freely when he was not fouling. Also on that squad were Jerry "Swish" Soltys and Dick "Vodra" Dworakowski, both pretty fair journeyman-type players, who had to back up the legendary Zuke Morris and Sonny Stook, two stalwarts who had previously performed for Joe Stepanik's Golden Pheasant squad. When it came time to quit the court scene, both Bewick and Farrington became accomplished marathoners. Furthermore, "Shoes" scaled all 46 peaks in the Adirondacks.

Then there was George Dixon. Originally, his fame lay with his long two-hand set shot – reminiscent of the great Zeke Sinicola of Niagara. George entered the modern era when he developed a one handed jumper from the corner - at the same time that he pioneered the power forward position. A big guy, in fact an original aircraft wide body type, Dixon failed to make the Canisius College varsity after 7 or 8 attempts but he did play at THE high school, and continued his hard court prowess as a member of the legendary BAC ( Buffalo Athletic Club) team of 1956-57. His key set-up man was Jim Burke, more often remembered for his excellence at handball. "Burkee" played with dexterity and determination; in modern parlance, he had great athletic ability. Once Jim hung up his Keds he played a major role at the annual BAC sports banquets, bringing to Buffalo the likes of baseball great, Sweet Lou Pinella.

The BAC team also featured two ex-St Joes All Catholic stars, Charlie

Ganey, a clever playmaker and Big Ed Killeen, an tough Irishman, who, when battling the boards with the great Dixon - well - they looked like a couple of Boston Celtics. In that 14-wins perfect season, Dixon, the captain and chief spokesman for the team, uttered that memorable phrase: "that was a time I will never forget."

Another athlete of fleeting potential was John Christiano of the well-known Christiano (sanfalese) family. His brother Tony was a sparkplug of the Fallon Manhattan Cup championship team in 1956. John was a veritable hustler on the court, playing the game similar to the way his sons played hockey years later. John claims to have made 45 consecutive foul shots, no record exists. John recalls that he would take his uniform (shorts, t shirt, sweat socks and a $3.99 pair of PF flyers) to the Connecticut Street Armory, leave his street clothes and wallet on the sidelines, (stealing was not a normal activity in those days), and start bouncing the ball on one of the many courts in the armory. I recall when I first entered the giant edifice to play MUNY ball I was overwhelmed at the sheer size of the place. It seemed as though there were at least 48 courts – actually there were far fewer but for a wide-eyed youth, appearances could be deceiving.

Basketball was a heck of a lot of fun, could be played at many sites, costs were minimal, and games did not consume huge chunks of time, which meant that you could still do a little homework.

## Memorial Auditorium: A Treasured History
Originally printed May 2010

*Memorial Auditorium no longer exists on lower Main Street. But the legendary AUD will remain in the memories of tens of thousands who attended events, a wide variety of events, there for over half a century. Many sport teams, especially basketball and hockey, played there. But concerts, political shindigs, circuses, and ice shows were regularly on the schedule. The AUD is one of the truly legendary buildings in Buffalo's rich history.*

No doubt most After-50 readers heard about the demolition of the AUD last year. Several media stories attempted to recall the glorious history of the old edifice. They concentrated almost exclusively on the Sabres. I would be the first to agree that the Sabres have been the most valuable addition to the AUD since the roof was raised in 1970. But that is only half the story.

113

The AUD's history starts during the Great Depression. Buffalo, like the rest of the nation, was in bad financial straits in the 1930s. To help out, the Works Progress Administration, WPA, poured money into the city to build a new sports arena (the old Broadway Auditorium was decrepit).

The AUD officially opened in 1940. Cy Kritzer, the legendary sportswriter, soon thereafter christened it: "The Pretty Lady of Lower Main Street". The very first athletic event featured wrestler Ed Don George. During the following decades, the 12,000 seat arena (16,000 plus once the roof was raised) hosted a rich variety of athletic events.

For years the main attraction was the Canisius College basketball doubleheader program (second only to Madison Square Garden as the mecca of college basketball in the entire country). Niagara, St. Bona, and Canisius, the legendary Little Three, hosted the nation's top quintets. The mid 50s saw the Griffs make three consecutive NCAA regionals; fans in the 60s cheered All Americans Calvin Murphy and Bob Lanier. In 1991, Duke, led by Christian Laettner, played Canisius before the largest crowd, 16,279, ever to see a college game in Buffalo. A bonus in the old days: the bar/lounge just left of the Terrace Street entrance was popular with college students. Beer was legal for 18 year olds, one might start imbibing at halftime and wind up hours later at Denny Brinkworth's newest saloon on Lower Main St.

In the AUD's first three decades, the Buffalo Bisons of the American Hockey League played to sellout crowds while accumulating several Calder Cup championships – paving the way for the NHL Sabres. Wrestling too featured the country's best. Sunni War Cloud, Yukon Eric, Gorgeous George, and Ilio DiPaolo all thrilled the area's mat fans.

Some of the greatest names in the sport of boxing fought in the AUD, including Sugar Ray Robinson, Willie Pep, the Muscato Brothers, Rocky Graziano and Carmen Basilio, the onion farmer from Canastota, NY. A heavyweight championship bout featuring Ezzard Charles took place in 1950. Thousands watched the Golden Gloves every December. What 12-year-old kid could ever forget sitting in the upper grays, the cheap seats, peering through thick layers of cigarette smoke trying to watch some 18-year-old amateurs slug their way to glory a mile away, or so it seemed.

The Roller Derby was popular in the 40s. The circuses, Ringling Brothers, the Shriners, and Barnum and Bailey all provided a world of fun for area youngsters. So did the Ice Capades, and Disney on Ice.

The AUD even played a role in the Cold War. In the 1960s, a large Russian delegation visited Buffalo, hosted by Canisius College. I was privileged to be a part of that. The Russians visited classes, participated in seminars and assembled cultural exhibits in the exhibit rooms near the Terrace Street entrance. The Cold War actually thawed a little right before your eyes in Memorial Auditorium.

Concerts too were a major event. Sinatra and Presley both performed, as did Elton John and Neil Diamond.

Wendell Willkie, Republican presidential candidate in 1940, held a major rally there. Twelve years later, over 20,000, the largest AUD crowd ever, somehow managed to squeeze in to hear Dwight D. Eisenhower in his run for the nation's top office.

*Sellout crowd at AUD for Title 3 basketball, 1950*

# Basketball's March Madness
Originally printed April 2011

*Ah! March Madness – the NCAA basketball tournament - one of the year's pleasurable sports event, often despite loud mouth Dick Vitale. It rates right up there with the Super Bowl, World Series, Masters and Stanley Cup.*

Those colleges that make it to the Final Four, more often than not, are perennial basketball powers – the huge state schools and a few private ones (Duke) dominate year after year. They are all members of big conferences; they all have large on-campus arenas holding between 15,000 and 25,000 fans. Rarely, does a Cinderella team such as George Mason advance to the Final Four. As for our local teams, they just don't compete regularly at the highest level anymore.

It wasn't always that way. Remember the good old days, all you "After 50" Buffalo fans. Back in the 1940s and 50s the AUD with its Saturday night doubleheaders was the place to be. It was there that our locals competed successfully against the best.

Downtown Buffalo was bustling with excitement. Unlike today when a Canadian goose could waddle down Main Street in the evening without getting hit by a car. The bars, the theaters, the hotels, the restaurants – Buffalo had its own Great White Way. From Tupper to Lower Main street, yes, legendary Lower Main, that sordid district below the AUD, the area where drunken sailors off the lake boats and other sorts of ne'er do wells accumulated in the Hotel Detroit and other venues of ill repute. Downtown was where the legitimate action took place: The Roundtable, MacDoels, Laube's, the legendary bars in the big hotels - the Statler, the Buffalo and the Lafayette, the theaters - large and plush – Shea's Buffalo, Great Lakes, and Hippodrome, and the Lafayette and the 20th Century and the music bistros, especially jazz, like Jans, the Gayety, the Colored Musicians Club, the Royal Arms (or was it the Stratford Arms - not quite downtown).

On Saturday nights, especially in the decade following WWII, sellout crowds of 12,000 were commonplace. Year after year, the local quintets had winning seasons that included victories over nationally ranked teams. Leroy Chollet, Bobby MacKinnon, Zeke Sinacola, were household names.

The Memorial Auditorium doubleheader program was so successful in the 1940s that New York City sportswriters labeled it as second only to Madison

Square Garden as a Mecca for the best in college basketball.

Things began to change gradually in the 1950s. Big name Eastern teams still came to play but the era of the basketball powers from elsewhere coming to the AUD was pretty much over. However the Little Three (a non-conference conference?) had come into its own and right down to 1970 games featuring Canisius, Niagara and St. Bona drew boisterous, enthusiastic, standing room only crowds. Often, the overflow could be found in the AUD's first level bar. (Staunch fans like Klu, Vodra, and Mike Davis were happy as long as a courier from the upper blues came in to give up to date scores occasionally.) Hey, you only had to be 18 to order a Jenny or a Simon Pure (Ug that was bad stuff).

Each of the local teams had some outstanding seasons in the 50s and 60s. Led by the likes of Ed Fleming, Charlie Hoxie, Boo Ellis, Al Butler and of course Calvin Murphy, Niagara made 6 NIT appearances in the 1950s, did so again in 1961 and in 1970 played in the NCAA tournament. Taps Gallagher coached the Purple Eagles.

The Griffins were golden in the mid-50s with three consecutive NCAA appearances; Johnny McCarthy and Hank Nowak starred; Joe Curran was their mentor. The MacKinnon coached Griffs made the NIT finals in 1963 led by Tom Chester (North Tonawanda's gift to the AUD) and Billy O'Connor. John Morrison and Andy Morrison sparked the Griffs winning seasons in the late 1960s along with His Honor, Mayor Tony Masiello, and rough and ready Dennis Misko. *Bona is Now the Bonnies!?*

And in that era, the Bona Brown Indians appeared in seven NIT tournaments. Bona topped off its success with an NCAA tournament in 1968 following the remarkable undefeated 22- 0 season and then an equally outstanding feat, the Bonnies made the Final Four in 1970. Who knows that if it were not for the injury to Bob Lanier the Olean team might have been # 1 in the entire country? Other big stars were Bill Butler, the Stith Brothers, especially all American Tom, Whitey Martin and Fred Crawford. Bona had terrific coaches: Eddie Melvin, Eddie Donovan, and Larry Weise.

Not far behind was the University of Buffalo. The Bulls, led by two exceptional coaches, Mal Eiken and Len Serfustini, compiled a number of winning seasons, and participated in several post-season tournaments. Jimmy Horne was the dominant UB player of the 50s.

Recently Budd Bailey in the Buffalo News noted that 40 years ago the local fans packed the AUD to see the final duel between perhaps the two greatest players to ever play for the locals, Calvin Murphy and Bob Lanier. Bailey indicated that their swan song kind of marked the end of an era. Tough to disagree with that statement.

Like so much in life, things are just not like the ol' days, the heyday of college basketball, those golden seasons of the 40s – 60s in downtown Buffalo that are part of our mystical past. They have gone the way of the Central Terminal, the Kenmore Tavern, and the Bedell House on Grand Island and of course, Lerczak's.

## When Basketball Was Huge in Buffalo

Originally printed February 2012

*College basketball was huge, second only to Madison Square Garden in the late 40s-early 50s. Buffalo itself was still considered a Top 10 US city. Major railroads brought in famous teams from throughout the country. UB and St. Bona as well as Canisius and Niagara played a top brand of basketball against those teams before sellout crowds.*

Recently, three basketball players from the Canisius team of the 1940s passed away: John Krochmal (Tonawanda), a good role player; John DeLuca (Amherst), captain of the '51 team; and Hank O'Keefe, arguably one of the first big stars in local college basketball. Those deaths reminded me of a recent issue of a monthly publication magazine that commented on the sad performances in recent years of local sports, especially the Bills, Sabres, and college basketball. According to the article, the college game was never very successful in Buffalo. For one who has lived with college basketball for the past 70 years, and generally for the whole "After 50" crowd, that is manifestly untrue.

There was a time, following WWII, when all four local teams were good; in fact, they were so good that one or another would often be ranked in the nation's top 20 (Dunkel). It was a time when college basketball in Buffalo was the talk of the nation, when the AUD doubleheaders were second only to those in Madison Square Garden. The NYC press covered the AUD games and sang its praises. It was a time when the AUD was packed with 10-12,000 fans and sellouts occurred regularly. Oh, the AUD was not as big as many college arenas today; for example, Kentucky hosts 24,000 per game. But in the 40s, as the sport was just becoming an American obsession, the AUD crowd looked mighty huge.

Why? Why was local college basketball so successful at that time? There were a number of reasons.

The city itself, Buffalo, was important. Buffalo was big, exciting, and growing. It was 10th in population (now about 50th), the economy was dynamic, well-known entertainers flocked to downtown, and politicians were generally honest. The city was thriving. The city also had Memorial Auditorium, popularly known as the AUD, built as a project of the WPA.

When visiting teams arrived downtown, they were lodged in impressive hotels such as the Statler, Lafayette, and the Buffalo. Teams came by train. Air travel had not yet replaced the railroad. The trains came into Central Terminal, or the Lehigh Valley, or the D. L. and W. Buffalo was then the 2nd leading rail center in the United States. Trains carried teams from the Far West and the South, stopping in Buffalo for a game at the AUD. A day or so later, the teams and trains continued on to Madison Square Garden and sometimes on to Philadelphia for a third game. Thus, a California or Arizona quintet could build up its non-conference schedule with a two-week trip East.

Buffalo also had Doc Crowdle, Canisius chemistry professor and Director of the AUD program. Canisius managed the AUD program; Niagara was integral to it, while Bona and UB played less frequently. Crowdle hooked up with Ned Irish who ran Madison Square Garden. Teams loved to play in NYC; exposure there might help gain a berth in the NIT, then the premier post-season basketball tournament. Crowdle and Irish scheduled top-flight competition; they became virtual impresarios of college basketball.

There were other reasons accounting for the Golden Age of college basketball.

The local institutions hired first-rate coaches; Canisius had Earl Brown, followed by Joe Niland (NYC press called Niland one of the brightest young coaches in the U.S.), Niagara had the legendary Taps Gallagher, Bona had Eddie Milkovich (a.k.a. Melvin), and Mal Eiken coached the UB Bulls.

And the players – wow, there were some great ones – some All–Americans, and many near-greats.

The Golden Griffins suited up O'Keefe, Leroy Chollet, Don Hartnett, Mort O'Sullivan, Larry O'Connor, and the premier local high school player of his day, "Black Rock" Bobby MacKinnon. Playing for the Purple Eagles of Niagara were Zeke Sinicola, Larry Costello, Tom Birch, Harry "the Horse" Foley, Ed Fleming and Charlie Hoxie. The Brown Indians of Bona had Kenny Murray,

Eddie Donovan, Sam Urzetta and Bob Sassone. UB stars included Len Serfustini, Jack Chalmers, Benny Constantino, and Lou Corriere. UB football ace Eddie Gicewicz logged some quality time on the basketball court.

Buffalo fans were able to watch several visiting All-Americans. They included Dolph Schayes of NYU, Don Barksdale of UCLA, Arnold Ferrin of Utah, Fred Schaus of West Virginia, Kevin O'Shea of Notre Dame, Easy Ed McCauley of St Louis, and Bob Cousy of Holy Cross. Southern Cal's Bill Sharman, St John's Bob Zawoluk and Dick Groat of Duke also played in the AUD.

Excellent players on top ranked teams visited Buffalo and played against equally excellent star-studded local teams and their respected coaches.

✳ The result: Buffalo's golden era of college basketball.

In the five-year period from 1946-51 (a total of 20 seasons for the 4 local teams), there were 17 winning seasons. Many of the teams that left town winless were not exactly creampuffs. Among those that were defeated by the locals were LSU, Syracuse, Arizona, Georgetown, California, Utah, Notre Dame, SMU, Duke, Texas, West Virginia, St John's, USC, Kansas State, Oregon State, Arkansas, Baylor, and more. Impressive? You bet.

The demise of this golden era began in 1951 when gambling scandals rocked the college basketball world. Centered in NYC, they spread throughout the land, even to Baron Rupp's Kentucky Wildcats. WNY was not directly involved but the impact of the scandals was felt widely; college attendance slipped. Western teams were reluctant to venture into the Babylon on the Hudson anymore. Local scheduling suffered.

✳ But other factors also accounted for changes in college basketball. Air travel replaced railroads. Teams from the west could now bypass Buffalo and simply fly into and out of an East Coast city consuming only 2-3 days travel.

In the early 1950s, Americans purchased that new sensation, the television set, by the millions. Now some erstwhile fans might sit home and watch a big game "on the tube" rather than don winter clothes and venture to downtown Buffalo.

There have been years when UB, Canisius, Bona, and Niagara have individually been very good. The three NCAA Canisius teams of the mid 50s were outstanding, as were the later Niagara and Bona teams of Calvin Murphy and Bob Lanier. Teams coached by Satalin, Layden, and Beilein all had their moments in the sun. But there was never an era similar to that which followed WWII.

There are still those who yearn for "the old good days." Well, like the 5-cent cigar, or the 10-cent cup of coffee at Decos, like most things in life, the good old days will not return.

**LEAPIN' LEROY ADDS TWO**

—Mott
Chollet is surrounded by Tigers as he scores in the second half against Louisiana State.

*"Leapin Leroy" Collet scores two points, swhile urrounded by rival Louisiana State*

Photo by Mott
MacKINNON SCORES, SURROUNDED BY NIAGARA'S JOHNSTON (26), MORAN (21), BIRCH (11) AND SMYTH (27)
*That one Last point*

*Bob MacKinnon, All time Canisius Great, leads the Griffs over archrival Niagara*

121

# A Trip to the AUD, Early 1950s
Originally printed January 2016

> *In the decade after WWII, a trip to Memorial Auditorium was a grand experience. Fans would take the streetcar (ended in 1950) or a bus down Main Street passing some of Buffalo's iconic buildings, passing the large movie palaces and multi-storied department stores and then walking from Shelton Square to the AUD. The main attractions included Canisius-Niagara basketball doubleheaders, often sold out, and often-featuring top 20 teams.*

Who has not heard about the revitalization of Buffalo? The News and other media regularly feature stories on Buffalo's plans and successes. Spree magazine's latest issue reviews the incredible progress since the turn of this century, including the Buffalo Niagara Medical Campus, Canalside, and the inner and outer harbor.

Across the country, Buffalo's progress is observed. A case in point: Some 55 years ago, three of my friends left the area and followed Jack Kerouac's road out West. We still keep in touch (that internet is great!). All three, Klu, Brow, and Vodra, are eager to know how things have changed in their old city, since the 1950s. Klu pined for the trips downtown to the AUD to watch the legendary Canisius – Niagara basketball doubleheaders. So I decided to oblige with an imaginary nostalgic journey.

We hopped on a streetcar (last one ran in 1950) at the Virgil Loop. Others (Fring, Shoes, Frugal Sid and Fast Adrian) joined the party. Down Parkside we traveled, past the Park Meadow and the legendary Cardina's General Store and then down Main Street.

As the trolley traveled past Ferry Street, Vodra looked out one side and said, "That's where the Headquarters for the 37 Deco restaurants stood." (Gone, now lofts?). Klu looked the other way and said, "Down there a couple of blocks, was Offermann Stadium where I watched Luke Easter and Vic Wertz." (Gone, now a school).

The streetcar clanged past Best Street: the "Brow" pointed East noting that "Civic Stadium was just a few blocks away, where we all watched the Original Buffalo Bills (Ratterman, Mutryn) play." (Gone, now Wiley Field). Next we passed where the large IRC (predecessor of NFTA) building stood. Fring remarked that is where you went to see if they had found your scarf or gloves you left on the bus.

We continued on to Tupper Street, the unofficial beginning of downtown Buffalo.

On the right was Bafo's, a late night place where Town Casino stars, e.g. Rosemary Clooney, imbibed after hours. Nearby were Noah's Ark, Western Auto and a huge army surplus store (where you bought the good stuff for Boy Scout camp) and also Dick Fisher's, Buffalo's famous sporting goods store. (Tell the clerk where you went to school – you got an automatic discount, even if the school was non-existent).

We past some high-end stores, Oppenheim-Collins, Flint and Kent, and Bergers, and arrived at Lafayette Square (kind of like Buffalo's Herald Square!) We pictured the old Library (replaced) on the far side. Voyer remarked that "often a reprobate was found loitering in the basement stacks, probably not doing research." Also on the square were The Hotel Lafayette (recently enhanced), where the St. Bona team stayed when visiting the AUD and Kleinhans, billed as the nation's (or world's?) largest men's store.

The trolley was cruising along Buffalo's "Great White Way," an area much smaller than Times Square, but with some cachet of its own. Laube's Old Spain, and MacDoels were landmarks. But it was the theaters that lit up Main Street. Vodra, in his well-known excitable delivery, did the narration. He recalled how Shea's Big Three dominated the scene: The Hippodrome (Center) and the Great Lakes (Paramount), (both gone) and the granddaddy of all, Shea's Buffalo, fortunately preserved. Basils Lafayette was a block away on Washington Street and nearby was The Century, itself, a rather grand theater.

We rolled past the big department stores: AM&As, Wm. Hengerer's, Hens & Kelly's and JN Adams, and arrived at the end of the line, Shelton Square (no more). Shelton Square was the final destination of many busses and trolleys. In the center of the Square was a weather shelter; downstairs was a sordid men's room.

Some noteworthy establishments surrounded Shelton Square (all gone now). Included were the Hotel Niagara, (definitely not a 5 star hotel), the Erie County Savings Bank, and on Main street were Bond Clothes (Your suit with two pants), Foody's bar, Mathias Cigar store, where one purchased tickets for all sporting events, and where bookies regularly made quick stopovers and the Palace.

The legendary Palace Burlesk! Klu offered some vivid memories of the patrons of the Palace. These included students coming of age, a few businessmen with hats furtively pulled down shading their faces, assorted characters shabbily attired, some regulars who told their wives that they came to hear the comedians and a few, like the Sweeney Boys, who claimed they went for the prize in the cracker jack box. Such prizes might include a two-bit Yo-Yo, or a miniature flashlight with dull batteries. (Value - priceless).

Our gang alighted from the #9 car, and hiked the remaining few blocks to the AUD. We ambled past the mammoth Ellicott Square Building and past the Hotel Worth, where truckers sacked out, and where post game beer blasts were held. As we neared the entrance to the AUD, our eyes focused on Lower Main, the "street of lost dreams". Denny Brinkworth, briefly, ran a saloon at the beginning of Lower Main. That was next to the Lehigh Valley Terminal. At the very end of Main was another railroad station, the D L& W. The terminals were the bookends for the infamous Lower Main. In between were flop houses, Seamen's homes, a greasy spoon serving coffee all night, a couple of gin mills, houses of ill repute and other memorable edifices. The Brow said, "Indeed, it was the Queen City's skid row," our answer to NYC's Bowery.

Finally, inside the AUD, we cheered on the Canisius and Niagara teams as they contested with some of the nation's best. At halftime we often wandered into the AUD's first floor bar (forgot the name). If the game was a bore, we stayed, belting down Black Labels and Jenny's, until the game was over, the lights dimmed, and we were ushered out.

We might find out later that it had been a great night for the local teams. An AUD capacity crowd of 12,000, not uncommon in those days, had watched as Don Hartnett pulled down rebounds and Bobby MacKinnon ran the offense. The result: the Griffs knocked off highly ranked Duke. Niagara, meanwhile, on a two-handed 35-foot set shot by Zeke Sinicola, beat West Virginia.

The fans fanned out to the Buffalo neighborhoods. Our gang trailed Mike Davis to the Everglades (eventually ending up, as usual, at the Golden Pheasant), Joe Bieron and his Kensington/Bailey pals headed for Bailo's, the South Buffalo contingent, Dick Robinson, Dan Sullivan, went to Dubels (if, with date) or to Mischlers or the Early Times. West Siders might stop at the Armory.

Ah, those were the good ol' days!

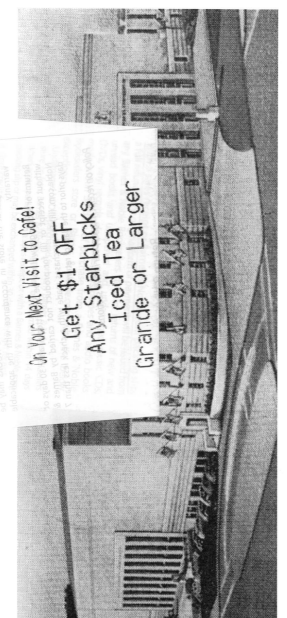

On Your Next Visit to Cafe!

Get $1 OFF
Any Starbucks
Iced Tea
Grande or Larger

*Memorial Auditorium – "The AUD" Buffalo's legendary sports arena*

# Chapter 7. Some Other Sports

*Football had always been a favorite sport in WNY. College and High School football was surprisingly popular in the post World War II years. The battle for the Harvard Cup, symbol of the Buffalo High School champion, was played on Thanksgiving Day before thousands at All High stadium. Later the Sabres and Bills took the spotlight shared briefly with the NBA Braves. Our local teams stuck with "basic" nicknames, rather than select some exotic offbeat moniker.*

## Two Pro Sports in a Mid-Size City- How can that be?
Originally printed June 2016

*Several cities, larger than Buffalo, do not have even one major professional sports team. Buffalo has two; the Sabres and Bills. For a brief period the city had three; the NBA Braves.*

A recent issue of Sports Illustrated mentioned expansion of the Big 4 pro leagues: Baseball, Basketball, Hockey and Football. The story cited the 10 most populous US cities without a team in at least one of the four major sports.

**Those teamless ten are:**

| | |
|---|---|
| Austin   912,791 | Fresno   515,986 |
| Las Vegas   613,599 | Va. Beach   450,980 |
| Louisville   612,780 | Omaha   446,599 |
| Albuquerque   557,169 | Colo. Springs   445,830 |
| Tucson   527,972 | Tulsa   399, 682 |

Buffalo's latest census shows a population of 258, 703. All ten listed above are larger. Even if one considers metro areas, the census indicates that Metro Buffalo falls in the middle of those ten. They range from Las Vegas with 2,114,000 to Albuquerque with 907,000. Buffalo comes in at 1,135,000.

What is the point? Buffalo is very fortunate to have not one but TWO pro sport teams (or some taxpayers might say unfortunate). Buffalo in the 21st century is a Big Little city, or better stated: A Big – Mid Size City.

## A Segue

40 years ago Buffalo had three major sports franchises, the third being the Buffalo Braves. The NBA Braves came on the scene at the same time that Buffalo's AHL Bisons morphed into the NHL Sabres.

Surprisingly, the three teams did quite well for a few years. The Sabres packed the newly roofed Memorial Auditorium regularly with some 16,000 fans. The Bills packed War Memorial and, then beginning in 1973, the Orchard Park stadium to capacity. The Braves drew very respectable crowds in the AUD.

Even more surprising was that this phenomenon was occurring at a time when the City of Buffalo was in a downspin. Our rustbelt city began to lose business and industry at an accelerating rate in the late 60s. Population followed suit. Buffalo's population went from a high in 1950 of 580,000 to 462,000 in 1970 and down to 357,000 in 1980.

With the population plummeting, with fewer people in the stands for some events (Braves) and with business leaving for the Sunbelt which meant fewer advertising dollars and less corporate support to provide much needed backing for the teams, the future was not rosy. This was occurring at a time when costs for players and owning a pro franchise were escalating.

The Braves left town in 1978. A recent two-part story in the Buffalo News discussed the Buffalo NBA teams (1970-78). It recalls the good old days. It also focuses on one time owner, Paul Snyder and the loss of the franchise.

There were some stellar moments in those pro basketball years. Old time fans like Gary Warner, Chuck Mancuso, and the entire Shatzel gang were thrilled to cheer on Jack Ramsay, Ernie D and Bob MacAdoo as well as Adrian Dantley, Bob Kauffman, and of course Randy Smith. Fans anxiously awaited the stories filed by Ace Sports Reporter Milt Northrup, especially those on the Braves and Celtics games played before huge crowds in the downtown arena.

Unfortunately, those halcyon days would not and could not last. Why not?

Why did the Braves leave?

Among other reasons suggested, the Buffalo News in a sub headline states: "Scheduling conflict at the AUD was insurmountable hurdle." The Braves claimed that they were not able to lock up an "adequate" number of Saturday nights.

### Here was the situation in the 1970s:

The City of Buffalo Contract gave the Sabres their choice of dates, which usually meant that the hockey club reserved Sundays and a weekday night for home games.

Canisius College, with a contract since the AUD first opened in 1940, had a hold on Saturdays during the college basketball season (usually 14 dates)

The Braves proceeded to play on Fridays, other weekend nights and Saturdays when available. The NBA season contained 22 Saturday dates (later 26). The Braves did play some Saturday nights in the AUD, and also played a number of Saturday road games.

1978!

### In the Braves era, 1970-78 the AUD Saturday situation was this:

| Years | Saturdays Available | Used by Canisius | Remaining | Used by Braves |
|-------|---------------------|------------------|-----------|----------------|
| 1970-71 | 22 | 13 | 9 | 8 |
| 1971-72 | 22 | 13 | 9 | 8 |
| 1972-73 | 22 | 14 | 8 | 7 |
| 1973-74 | 22 | 12 | 10 | 7 |
| 1974-75 | 22 | 11 | 11 | 8 |
| 1975-76* | 26 | 8 | 18 | 12 |
| 1976-77 | 26 | 7 | 19 | 10 |
| 1977-78 | 26 | 7 | 19 | 12 |

*NBA season expanded*

As Director of Athletics, I worked on the AUD schedule exclusively with Joe Figliola, the Director of the AUD. Canisius was moving away from of a full component (14) of Saturday nights in the AUD. Canisius began playing an occasional game in the on-campus gym (1975). Also Bona opted to play only of its two annual games with Canisius in the AUD, the other at the Reilly Center. Niagara followed suit when the Niagara Falls Convention Center opened in 1973. Two more Saturdays were available for the Braves! Also about this time,

Canisius eliminated the Queen city Tournament. Another Saturday opened up. Obviously more Saturday nights available for the Braves!

There were several factors involved in the demise of the Braves in Buffalo. The Saturday issue sometimes cited as the most important was just one of several factors. In fact, that factor was decreasing in importance.

More important was the fact that there was simply not enough financial or demographic support left in rustbelt Buffalo to support three major sport franchises.

A decade after the Braves left, a sparkling new baseball stadium was built in downtown Buffalo. Some optimists hoped that Buffalo might land a MLB franchise; the sport was ripe for expansion. Ten cities (areas) were in the mix. Buffalo did not have a chance. The April 1989 issue of Athletic Business placed Buffalo as #10, citing "negative population growth" as key. Bob Rich breathed a sigh of relief.

*Buffalo Braves All Stars: Ernie D. plays with the big boys, Kareem Abdul Jabbar*

# Zuke's Sports Update – of Many Years Ago
Originally printed February 2013

*The legendary Sports enthusiast Zuke recalls some of the great moments in Buffalo's sports history especially the OLD Buffalo Bills in Civic Stadium led by George Ratterman. Zuke, also comments on Football bowl games and college basketball in the AUD.*

Ran into an old pal recently, Paul Morris, aka "Zuke" or "The Zuker." Zuke was anxious to fill me in with his latest sports observations:

Naturally, he began with the Bills, "Yeah, I know they need a QB, the one they have reminds me of Gary Marangi. Remember him? He completed a lot of passes, but mostly to the opposition." The Bills haven't had a good one since Doug Flutie. Kelly of course was the best, Ferguson and Kemp were good. And the mad bomber, Darryl Lamonica, gave us some thrills before he took off for Super Bowl bound Oakland.

I reminded the Zuker of the days in the late 40s when we sat with Fring and Shoes near the tunnel in Civic Stadium and watched the old Bills of the AAFC. We were avid George Ratterman fans. Zuker added: "now there was a guy with potential, old 'sleight of hand' Ratterman". At 20, in 1947, he tossed 22 TDs, a record for a professional football rookie. He led Buffalo to its first playoff game – a victory over Baltimore in 1948. Great all-around athlete at Notre Dame: baseball, tennis, basketball (played against Canisius in the AUD). After the Bills were "dumped" by the NFL, Ratterman headed for the best team in all football, the Cleveland Browns, as an understudy for the greatest QB of his era, Otto Graham. Upon Otto's retirement in 1956, Ratterman took control, even made the cover of a new magazine, Sports Illustrated; alas, a few weeks later he experienced a career ending injury.

By this time, the Zuker and I were sitting on our favorite barstools at the Golden Pheasant. While Joe the Bartender, poured a couple Jenny drafts (10 cents each), our conversation continued. Zuke said the only solution was to exhume Bobby Layne, a splendid QB as well as a favorite of the saloon crowd. He added that perhaps the Bills could locate Buckets Hirsh and Mike Stratton (60s) to beef up the linebacker corps.

We moved on to the Bills' stadium situation. After a colorful string of obscenities against the NFL for its abuse of low-income taxpayers, Zuke suggested that a new stadium should be put in the middle of Broadway – right between where Sattlers (998) and the Polish Village used to thrive. The entire area now looked like Dresden just after WWII. Zuke's frequent drinking companion, Sonny Stooch added his two cents, suggesting that the stadium be constructed on the hallowed site of the Broadway market BUT, with the proviso that butter lambs and Polish hams could be sold at Eastertime. Gotta keep the old parishioners from Corpus Christie and St Stan's happy, as well as their Cheektowaga descendants who make the nostalgic trip to the market each year. Besides, it seemed a better idea than building a stadium on the frigid lakefront.

We moved to the Bowl games and I reminisced how New Year's Day in the 1950s was a festive occasion. We would watch the Orange, Sugar, Cotton and finally the Rose Bowl games. Now what do you have? 30 some bowl games played over a 3-4 week period with such endearing names as the Go Daddy Bowl, and The Famous Idaho Potato Bowl. (Is there a lowly Maine Potato Bowl) and the Beef O'Grady Bowl. (No Beef on Weck bowl yet). Well I said I have no objection to all those bowl games. Zuke groused a bit, but I said that football is so commercialized now why not all those games to give hundreds of football players a chance for some later nostalgic pride as in "Hey I played in (or warmed the bench) at the Bell Helicopter Armed Forces Bowl."

By this time we had worked our way down the avenue to Klippels (Kenmore & Delaware) - a saloon Zuke fondly remembered, having been "served" there at the ripe old age of 15 ( Fake draft cards were easy to come by). The subject switched to basketball. Zuke loved that sport ever since some 55 years ago, as a member of the Canisius HS Acrions, (kids under 5' 3") he played between halves at the Memorial AUD doubleheader program. The Zuker was an ornery scrapper, not afraid to clock some bigger guy who blocked his way to the basket.

Those great doubleheaders are a thing of the past. That old cliché, "the only thing certain is change (?) or something like that" - Zuke muttered. Seems true enough in the world of sports! We had much more to talk about, especially the improving local basketball scene but that would have to wait another day. Zuke ordered one more for the road; at the same time he asked Joe Duff, the bartender, if he could "hold a sawbuck" until their paths crossed again.

As we parted ways, I told Zuke our discussion reminded me a little of the late, great Mike Royko and his pal, Slats Grobnik. Royko was the legendary, award winning Chicago columnist. "After 50" types should remember him. Zuke recalled that Royko rose to fame in the 1960s largely through his efforts to expose the problems of Mayor Richard Daley's Chicago. Indeed his book, "Boss," all about Daley's venal city, was a minor-classic. Zuke was especially pleased because Royko seemed to be in the tradition of the great H. L. Mencken of the Baltimore Sun. "Shoes" had indoctrinated Zuke and all the Barons with Mencken mania. More on that at another time!

*Civic Stadium – later War Memorial – Home of original Buffalo Bills*

## Joe Namath - Most Influential QB - Ever??
Originally printed February 2011

*In the 1960s, quarterback Joe Namath was not only a highly regarded football player but one of the country's top celebrities. He symbolized the decade of the 60s and became a legend.*

A month ago award winning Buffalo News sports columnist Jerry Sullivan selected his five greatest quarterbacks of all time. It's tough to disagree with his choices. Tom Brady topped the list, followed by Otto Graham (first choice of sports guru, Dr. Tom Banchich), Joe Montana, John Elway, and Johnny Unitas. Appropriately, the QBs starred in different eras, i.e. Graham just after WWII, Unitas in the years that followed, Montana in the 70s-80s, Elway in the fin de siècle, and Brady in the first decade of the present century.

Nowadays we have mountains of statistics to back up "Who was the greatest?" Still, differences of opinion abound. Was Bart Starr (no relation) better than Unitas? What about Bret Favre, Dan Marino, and Peyton Manning? And Jim Kelly, Troy Aikman, Terry Bradshaw! There is a place for all of them in a top 10, or the best 25. J P Losman or Trent Edwards would not make the list. Even the three amigos: Rick Hammond, Dave Dengler, and Charlie Durante agree on that.

One can marshal the huge data available to support who's best, top, and greatest! Most passes completed, most touchdowns, fewest interceptions, most yards gained, most big games won, most championship rings, and on and on to absurdity, e.g. most times a great QB threw to the left side of the field between the 5 and 10-yard line while wearing a cast on his big toe.

Those adjectives - GREATEST, BEST, TOP mean pretty much the same thing, but they do not necessarily mean influential.

Phil Taylor, in a recent Sports Illustrated issue writes about how we might better rate top athletes, e.g. Hall of Famers. He has St Peter as the gatekeeper doing the judging. Taylor notes that in some cases, athletes with excellent stats might be kept out. BUT adds Taylor: "The Gatekeeper is much more interested in whether the player created a lasting legacy in the sport." That translates to: INFLUENTIAL. Paraphrasing Webster's Dictionary: INFLUENTIAL - effective, persuasive, power to affect others – having impact on the sport and on society in general.

Who was the most influential QB in the NFL? Joe Namath wins - hands down. The stats freaks might be aghast - "Namath! - are you a lunatic?"

Okay. Namath did have some good credentials: an all-star selection, eventually a Pro Football Hall of Fame inductee, first QB to throw for 4000 yards in a season. But – not on a level with those QBs rated "best" or "Greatest." Fine, that is what stats will do. But let's look at influence.

Namath was selected first in the 1965 college draft by the American Football League. The NFL passed on him as "too expensive." BUT Sonny Werblin of the AFL New York Jets signed him for the unheard of sum of $400,000, actually $427,000, a record at that time. Today first round draftees sign for tens of millions, sums that now appear almost meaningless. Back in the mid-60s, $427,000 was astounding. And influential!

The Namath contract made the football world (including the curmudgeon NFL owners) aware that the AFL meant business. The upstart league was here to stay. The merger wheels picked up momentum – the AFL and NFL became the AFC and NFC under the NFL umbrella. The Namath signing proved extremely influential.

Still the old league, the senior NFC, continued to sneer at the "lowly" AFC. Perhaps with some justification as the Packers whipped the Chiefs then the Raiders in the first two super bowls.

Then – 1969 – Super Bowl III, Namath's Jets versus the redoubtable Baltimore Colts. Coach Shula's Unitas lead team was judged to be even stronger than the Packers. Very few gave the Jets the slightest chance. But Joe Namath did. Three days before the game he asserted "we are gonna win the game. I guarantee it." The Jets did. In one of the greatest upsets in NFL history, Namath picked apart the Colts vaunted defense. When asked afterwards if Baltimore had the best defense he faced, he answered, "No, that would be the Buffalo Bills defense."

There is still more to the Namath legend, the Namath influence.

Namath was a product of the 1960s, the most tumultuous decade in American history, highlighted by antiwar Vietnam protests, free speech convulsions, civil rights revolutions, (At Alabama , Namath even got into fights with white southerners while defending blacks), and feminist issues. Those were years of upheaval, even in lifestyles, dress, hair, and more. Namath symbolized the times with his own iconoclasm. With long black hair (no jock style crew cut for him) wearing a fur coat on the sidelines, playing in white sneakers, Namath was a virtual culture icon. Joe was even more influential because he played on the world's biggest stage, Gotham, the Big Apple. Broadway Joe, he was labeled – quite appropriate. Part of that stage included Bachelors III, an upscale Manhattan bar, of which he was part owner – briefly. Still the episode enhanced the Broadway Joe legend.

Shortly thereafter when it came time for Monday Night Football (it would become the longest running TV sports program in history); you guessed it: Namath and the Jets were automatics for the inaugural.

Was Joe Namath the greatest QB ever? No. Was he the most influential? Check it out.

*Joe Namath*

*Civic Stadium (Old Rock Pile) Football and many other sports played here - 1940s - 70s*

# Pro Sports Teams - What's in a nickname?

Originally printed November 2014

*Nicknames are universally popular – for food, friends, and all sorts of athletic teams. The Pros have a colorful variety: some funny, some goofy, some relevant, and some whatever!*

While looking over old stuff that we - pack rats - accumulate, I came upon a Mike Royko column about baseball nicknames. Mike was a popular, prize winning Chicago columnist. He had some great comments, which I use as a stepping-stone to comment on nicknames in all four major professional sports organizations.

In 1995, the Cleveland Indians faced the Atlanta Braves in the World Series. Politically correct dingbats took offense at the nicknames. Royko said he did not understand them, "because the players on these teams were not wearing feathers, grunting "ugh" or staggering from drinking too much firewater." Royko proceeded to suggest that several baseball teams might change their nicknames to more accurately depict the personality or ethnic makeup of the cities the teams represent.

He pointed out that The Brewers for Milwaukee, reflecting the local beer-making heritage, was a sensible nickname. Also: Orioles. Rangers, Yankees, and Nats – all seemed appropriate.

But how about the Los Angeles Dodgers. That made sense when the Brooklyn fans were dodging vehicles on their way to Ebbetts Field a hundred years ago. But for Los Angeles, Royko felt that the LA Loonies would be a better fit. Braves in Atlanta! No way. Reflecting its southern heritage, maybe the Atlanta team should be called the Rednecks. The St. Louis Cardinals! Well now that Gateway City to the West is not known for having flocks of bright colored birds nor for a host of Roman Catholic Cardinals. Would not the St Louis Godzicks be more indicative of the great fan loyalty of many of the Polish populace? The Pirates in Pittsburgh – there's a puzzling one. Have many Blackbeards been seen splashing around in the Monongahela and Ohio rivers, threatening local steel workers?

The National Basketball Association has some "legitimate" ones: Pacers, Celtics, Suns, 76ers - but also many stupid ones: Cavaliers, Mavericks, Wizards. The Raptors is goofy. Have these prehistoric beasts been seen in Toronto (no reference intended to Mayor Rob Ford). The Utah Jazz! A contradiction! It was fine as a nickname when located in New Orleans but in Salt Lake?? If the Utah team wants a musical nickname, how about the Utah Mormon Tabernacle Choirboys? Grizzlies for Memphis! There's a beauty! When was the last time anyone saw Grizzlies prowling Beale Street?

THE NFL has several meaningful nicknames: Packers, 49ers, Steelers, Vikings, Ravens (Edgar Allen Poe lived there). But several seem to have no meaning for the cities they represent: especially animal names like Bears in Chicago, Lions, Bengals, Rams, Falcons. Just dumb!

However a few animal names are appropriate: Timberwolves – there are some in Minnesota, Coyotes in Arizona - good.

Perhaps because many NHL teams are of more recent origin many of their nicknames do seem appropriate. A very questionable one: The Penguins! Was there a legendary Pittsburgher of Scandinavian origin named Rasmussen who once discovered Penguins playing ice hockey in Antarctica? If the Pittsburgh fans favor alliterations, would not Pugilists be suitable? Hockey players have been known to slug it out.

What about the monikers for our own teams in Western New York? The Buffalo Bills! William Cody earned that sobriquet Buffalo Bill for slaughtering about 4,280 Buffalos (Bison). Later he became a celebrity as he toured the country in his Wild West show. But Buffalo Bill was never seen in Delaware Park firing his rifle at the Buffalos in the local zoo! Still, it is a nifty nickname; I like it. And the charging Buffalo on the football helmets is one of the best in the NFL.

The Buffalo Sabres is another story. Are Buffalonians known for rattling swords? Is the sport of fencing popular throughout the Queen City? "They" say that Seymour Knox chose the nickname from some winning contest entries. Knox was universally admired as a great hockey owner and an even greater Buffalonian - but probably not a great nickname selector!

Finally, cities try to avoid having two teams using the same nickname. However and here is a great trivial question, worthy of the TV show, Jeopardy! Buffalo once had five of its sport teams all named the Bisons and all in the same year, 1946. Name them? Win a trip to Lackawanna and a beef on weck!

The first is obvious the Baseball Bisons. Many sports fans also will recall that before the Sabres, the hockey team also was the Buffalo Bisons.

The other three: in 1946 the AAFC, All American Football Conference, was formed. In its first year the Buffalo franchise was the Bisons. It was a horrible team. A contest was held in 1947 and the Buffalo Bills won out as the new nickname. It was a far better team and led to many of us embracing boy-hood heroes (or future legends): George Ratterman, Chet Mutyrn, and Buckets Hirsch.

The fourth Bison team in 1946 was Buffalo's professional basketball team. It was in one of the two pro basketball leagues then in existence. The NBA did not start until 1949. Incidentally, the Bison "roundball" quintet did not even make it through its first season.

The fifth- the champion Buffalo Roller Derby team was called the Bisons in 1946. It lasted a few years and actually won a championship. There was both a men's and a women's team. The women were especially popular; there are still a few gray-haired Buffalo fans who recall the dynamics of Captain Gerry Murray and her squad.

Americans love nicknames, No doubt about that! There are plenty of colorful, and many absolutely absurd, nicknames for college and high school teams throughout our fair land. That's a whole other story.

*George Ratterman, Bills' First Great Quarterback*

# Harvard Cup: A Thanksgiving Tradition
Originally printed October 2010

*Today High School athletic teams have numerous classifications, even more all-star teams, and countless trophies to be won by players and teams. But in the mid-20th century, the Harvard Cup stood alone; it was symbolic of the best High School football in the area.*

The Harvard Cup – more than 100 years old – is no more. The Buffalo Public High schools that competed for that prize will now play in Section VI in Western New York.

The Harvard Cup was a Thanksgiving Day ritual. I remember it well. Early Thanksgiving morning, hours before the big bird was carved, the best of the Buffalo High Schools played for the CUP. Sometimes it snowed, more often a gray, damp, dismal November day, but fans, by the thousands, turned out.

The first one I recall was at the end of World War II. McKinley Vocational was the powerhouse then. The McKinley Macks were led by stars like Chet Kwasek and Les Molnar. They ran roughshod over all opponents while chalking up 4 consecutive championships. My brother, Jim, played for McKinley so I had a vested interest.

The Harvard Cup dates from the earliest days that the Buffalo city high schools played football, the 1900s (suburbs were virtually nonexistent at that time). In the first Harvard Cup championship in 1904, Masten Park defeated Central (later Hutch-Tech).

But why a cup named for Harvard? One may wonder, in this modern age of football giants such as USC, Florida, Ohio State, Texas, Alabama, - why Harvard? Why the Harvard Cup?

At the turn of the century, 1900, not long after football was conceived, the Big Three in college football were Harvard, Yale, and Princeton. They were the first to play before tens of thousands of spectators and to participate in what became a Traditional Thanksgiving day game in New York City. Decades later, those schools joined others in what became known as the Ivy League and decided to deemphasize football. But in the early 20th century, Harvard was a power and it was appropriate that the championship in Buffalo would have a trophy named after the renowned institution.

In Buffalo, the first Harvard Cup dynasty was Lafayette. From 1906 through 1915, the Violets won all but one championship. In the 1920s, Masten

Park was the dominant school. By the end of the 30s Bennett emerged as the class of the league; in the mid-40s it was McKinley's turn. Then came Kensington, under its great coach, Wilbur Bergstrom. The Knights accumulated four straight titles, piling up 87 points to a mere 7 for the opposition. East High School strung together four championships in the mid-1950s; the Dingboom juggernaut followed. Charley Dingboom, an inductee in this year's Greater Buffalo Sports Hall of Fame, coached his Riverside team to an enviable five consecutive titles. From 1962-66, paced by Joe Ehrmann, later an All American at Syracuse and a star for the Baltimore Colts, the Riverside Frontiers were invincible.

In the decades that followed, several teams had their moment in the sun. The most dominant probably was Grover Cleveland. Throughout the 70s, 80s, and 90s, the President's eleven was at the top of the league. In recent years, McKinley and a few others have been successful in the run for the cup.

Some exceptional players, coaches, officials and administrators are now in the Harvard Cup Hall of Fame including Mark Lyles of Grover, Nipper Castine of Kensington, Orv Cott, Sr. of East, Al Dekdebrun of Burgard, George Voskerschian, Msgr. John Zeitler and Don Gilbert of Bennett, and Dr. Ed Gicewicz of Technical. Charles Monan, the promoter behind the largest crowd ever to witness a high school game in local football history (some say in the entire nation's history) is enshrined in the Hall – 50,988 fans turned out for the Kensington-Bennett game at Civic Stadium in October of 1948.

The Harvard Cup championship games were held in All High Stadium since it first swung open its gates in the late 1920s. It was constructed directly behind the newly opened Bennett High School. Under the guidance of Athletic Director, Dave "Driving Force" Thomas, All High Stadium has recently been renovated. Previously Thomas had been a tennis phenomenon at Kenmore High and Bradley University and taught the game at Sugarloaf in Canada. Nowadays Dave is aiming at golf records at Park Club in his bid to make the Senior PGA circuit. Dave had a long successful tenure in the Buffalo school system and it is fitting that he has over seen the stadium's rebirth just before he announced his richly deserved retirement this past spring. All High is as good as ever and will surely accommodate many football games in the future sans Harvard Cup.

Superintendent James Williams made the decision for the Buffalo high schools to join the Section VI football federation this season. Now different

Buffalo high schools will be playing different opponents from throughout Western New York. Chances are the city teams will be competitive.

The Buffalo Gridders, who play in Depew Stadium, will have the unique opportunity to hear one of the games legendary play-by-play announcers. "Spider" O'Neil has been at the microphone at that site for half a century. O'Neill is celebrated for injecting into his announcing Classical references (e.g. "looks like Aristophanes, or was it Socrates, performed on that last play") liberally spiced with an exuberant vocabulary perhaps matched only by the late Howard Cosell.

So no more Harvard Cup on Thanksgiving – the end of a century old tradition. But changes are necessary to accommodate changing times. Life goes on.

## Mascots/Nicknames: A banana slug!
Originally printed March 2013

*College sport teams have adopted some funny and some really weird nicknames over the past century. A few were deemed politically incorrect but efforts to change them have not gone well.*

Nicknames/Mascots for sports teams! There are some beauties: colorful, bizarre, including an all-time favorite, The Banana Slugs. It's the nickname/mascot for the California/Santa Cruz men's teams. So along comes Title IX and what do they call the women's teams – "SLUGS", just "Slugs." Is that fair? I mean a female student might say "I have a date with a handsome Banana Slug tonight" whereas a male student counters with "I am very interested in that good looking slug?" Oh, well.

Nicknames change too, sometimes due to pressure from the "politically correct whackos" as my pal, Zuke, labels them. The PCers are ready to pounce again; ready to tackle Washington (NFL) for its nickname, Redskins. Some Indians find that offensive; a change is warranted, sounds okay. But with other Indian monikers, the PCers went too far. They (with the NCAA's blessing) hammered the North Dakota hockey team – the Fighting Sioux. But the Sioux Indians, themselves, voted approval of the nickname. If Notre Dame has its Fighting Irish, the Sioux can be honored too.

The PCers have been raising a rumpus with the NCAA for some time. (The Pros don't pay much attention to them, witness the Braves, Chiefs, and Indians). Colleges, influenced by leftist faculty and dimwitted administrators, are all too willing to surrender to the PC police. They almost won at Florida State on the Seminole issue, but the Indians themselves came to the rescue, keeping Chief Osceola as the mascot. Osceola, a fierce warrior, is proudly admired at Seminole home games.

Marquette caved in – the administration banished the "warriors" nickname despite overwhelming opposition from alumni and students. Now it's the Golden Eagles. The nickname of Eastern Michigan U. used to be the Hurons, but the Michigan Department of Civil Rights pressured a change. On the other hand, Central Michigan did it right. With the support of the local tribe, the moniker, Chippewas, was adopted and is respected by both the Indians and the university community.

Some years ago, a humorous list appeared in a trusted sport magazine, offering alternatives to the nicknames that offended the politically correct. These included: The Gettysburg College Bullets. PCers claiming bullets glorified violence suggested "Blanks" as an alternative. The "Lumberjacks," Humboldt State's nickname, was said to endorse the slaughter of the spotted owl, so change to Crackerjacks! Boilermakers (Purdue) - offered temptation to recovering alcoholics - substitute "The Shirley Temples," and the Whittier College Poets, an effete word - so substitute "The Insurance Salespersons." Yes the Whittier College Insurance Salespersons. Tough to believe that one! In all the above cases, the PCers lost out to common sense.

Here are some other recent changes: some funny, others just plain dumb. Often the gender issue in the hands of radical feminists became part of the politically correct agenda. How about Syracuse! They used to be called the Orangemen. Well, Orangewomen did not sound too swift, so the school went with just plain old Orange - as in a piece of citrus fruit. Wow, what an awesome nickname! I digress for a personal remembrance – Back in 1976 at the AUD in Buffalo, Canisius defeated the Orangemen (last time). At game's end, some nut way up in the blues fired an orange at a Syracuse player and hit him, the player winged it back up into the stands, Splat! A funny incident; maybe the nickname should be kept. Others refer to the Syracuse team as the CUSE - now ain't that a beauty? The CUSE, the Orange - Help – save us!

Close by is Ithaca College, once known as the Cayugas. That nickname was dropped and now Bombers is used. Faculty protested asserting martial overtones. Zuker muttered that a few fake grenades lobed at those faculty "pinkos" ought to wake them up to reality.

A few schools had Red as part of their nickname. Red smacked of the Commies, the Bolsheviks, decades ago. However, the real objection was because of the identification of "red" with Indian. Title IX may have been involved too. For example, the St. John's Redmen! Rather than opt for Redwomen, a novel solution was used (temporarily) namely the "Basketball Express". So the big question emerged for the volleyball team - How does this grab you? - The "St Johns Basketball Express Volleyball team" How clever? Maybe that was only hearsay. Actually, Red Storm became the new nickname. Okay Weather Channel's Al Roker and Stephanie Abrams, what is a red storm? Is there a blue storm?

The list goes on: unique, clever, colorful, and presumably noncontroversial and popular.

Akron Zips! A perennial favorite, always on a top 10 list! According to Akron expatriate, Pat Greenwald, the name comes from the zippers on boots made in Akron. It was also reported that for a while the school song, sung by Boom Boom and the Zip-a-longs was "Zip A Dee Do Dah", but fans could not agree on what a Doo Da was – so the song was dropped.

And how about those St. Louis Billikins! Inscrutable! So spell binding that fans still argue over what a Billikin really is. The Wichita State "Wheatshockers" - out on the Great Plains that nickname makes a lot of sense. One of the Arkansas colleges handled the gender issue nicely. The men were the Boll Weevils and so the women's teams became the Cotton Blossoms. Shrewd!

In 1950, about 20,000 fans showed up in a futile effort to save the Buffalo Bills from extinction. Then in 1970, the roof was raised and the Sabres were born. The NBA Buffalo Braves quickly followed. They did surprisingly well both on the floor and at the gate. Soccer also had a presence. In the late 70s, the Buffalo Stallions played; a few years the Buffalo Blizzard did. The Major Indoor Lacrosse league placed the Buffalo Bandits in the aging arena; they drew huge crowds.

In the years since the roof was raised, it was the Sabres that made the building famous. The French Connection, Jim Schoenfeld, Danny Gare, Pat LaFontaine, and Dominik Hašek all became household names in Western New York. Season after season sellout crowds were common. Just as the Raised Roof AUD was synonymous with the Sabres in the last half of the facility's existence, the early AUD, the original building was synonymous with College basketball in the 40s and early 50s, when many of the great All Americans and national powerhouses played in the AUD.

I recall vividly when I became Athletic Director in the 70s, attending NCAA meetings, where I would encounter legendary ball players and coaches of the old days from around the country who, at the drop of a hat, would reminisce about the great days in the AUD. The AUD had a national reputation and for different sports and at different times.

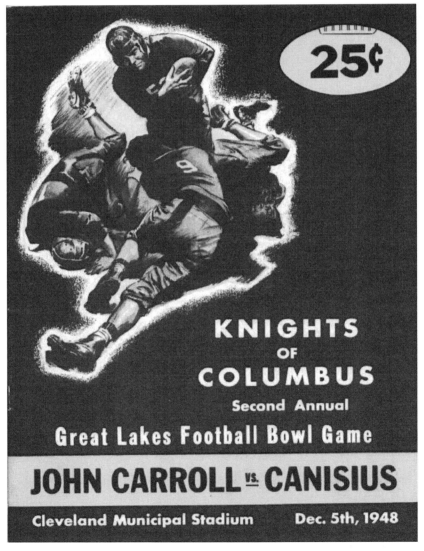

*Flyer for 1948 Knights of Columbus Great Lakes Football Game*

# Local College Football after WWII
Originally printed February 2010

*It may surprise young people, but college football played by Canisius, Niagara, Bona, and U.B. was very popular in the 1940s. Over 35,000 attended the Canisius-Bona game in 1946, the largest crowd to ever see a college game in WNY in the entire 20th century.*

It may seem incredible to those under 50 years of age, but Western New York in the 1940s was a hotbed for college football. All four local colleges: Canisius, St. Bonaventure, U.B. and Niagara, fielded competitive teams.

Good players abounded. Stroll through the hallowed halls of Alumni Arena at U.B. and you will see the picture of Lou Corriere, one of the school's great all around athletes. Lou was a terrific running back as was Sal Amico, who starred as halfback after Lou graduated. Sal went on to coach Fallon High School, and yours truly, in its very first year with a varsity program. Another legend was big Ed Gicewicz, a dominant end, who, in the years that followed, became an esteemed local physician. Jules Licata, Les Molnar, and many other local lads including Charley Dingboom, Matty Ferrentino, and Russ Gugino starred for the Bulls. Their success was seen in victories over rivals Alfred, Niagara, St. Lawrence, and the tough teams from Bucknell as well as a monumental upset over the University of Louisville.

The Purple Eagles from Niagara University also had some topnotch local talent. Quarterback John Theobald had starred at Kenmore High School. Dick Wojciechowski, a fleet end for the Purple Eagles, was a force in several victories. Dick McCarthy, a native of the Big Apple, starred at the center position. Bob Rosa, Walt Jankowski, Les Dugan (later coach at Buffalo State) and Nick Stojakovich also excelled for the Purple Eagles.

St. Bona, with Hugh Devore at the helm, recruited outstanding talent. A few of the players he had at Notre Dame during the war years followed him to Bona. Phil Collella had starred for the Fighting Irish in 1945. When he found himself at odds with Frank Leahy, Devore brought him to Olean where he, and Frank LoVuolo and "Mr. Smear," Mitch Smiarowski steamrolled a strong Bona team over top competition. Later Ted Marchibroda arrived at St. Bona. In 1950, he was the leading passer in Eastern College football. Later he served as offensive coordinator for the Buffalo Bills.

Bona fans packed Forness stadium on the campus. Capacity was listed at

8,000 seats, somehow more than 10,000 frequently attended. Among the Bona victims on the gridiron were St. Louis, Dayton, William and Mary, San Francisco and Boston University.

Meanwhile archrival Canisius College vied with St. Bona for top dog in WNY. Several legends emerged for the Golden Griffins. Big Jim Naples was a rugged receiver. Following his football career, Naples became one of Buffalo best known restaurateurs. He and George Steinbrunner of NY Yankee fame ran the Round Table, close by the Statler in downtown Buffalo. Naples was Buffalo's answer to Toots Shors.

Don MacKinnon, of the famous MacKinnon family of Black Rock, centered the Griffs offense. Bob Jerussi, a product of NYC, a solid lineman, was known to be "quick as lightning." A 17-year-old youngster from New Jersey, Howie Willis, came to be recognized as one of the greatest football players in Canisius history. In the backfield with him was Chet Kwasek, a product of powerful McKinley High School. The formidable Griffin forward line was anchored by George Eberle, Ray Jacobi, and George Kuhrt, perennial members of the all WNY football team. The backfield also starred Smiley Braatz, Jacques Austin and Nipper Castine.

Both Canisius and St. Bonaventure featured excellent teams in all four years immediately following World War II. The 1948 Golden Griffins were at the top of the list. Underscoring its excellence, the Canisius Football team of 1948 is being honored this winter with the induction into the Canisius Hall of Fame. It is a well-deserved award for a team with a record of 7 - 2 - 1 that earned a berth in the Great Lakes Bowl in Cleveland to face home town favorite John Carroll University. The John Carrol backfield featured Don Shula, who would become the winningest coach of the Miami Dolphins. His teammate was running back, Carl Taseff, who later played in the NFL and then, (here is one for the trivia buffs) Taseff was on the roster of one of the early Buffalo Bills teams of the AFL. In the bowl game, Canisius took an early lead. John Carroll pulled ahead and wound up with a 14 – 13 victory.

The Great Lakes Bowl was just one of several highlights. St. Bona also played in post season. In 1946 they lost by a point to Muhlenberg in the Tobacco Bowl in Kentucky. Fan Support was impressive both on the road and at home. In Civic Stadium in 1946, the Canisius-St. Bona contest drew more than 35,000 spectators, the largest crowd ever to witness a college game in the 20th century.

It all came to a sudden end. In January 1950, the Original Buffalo Bills went out of existence. A month later Canisius terminated its football program. A year later, NU did, and a year after that Bona followed suit. UB struggled on. Costs had skyrocketed for small colleges. All benefited from the return of the war veterans, but as those numbers dried up, enrollments shrank. And then television entered the picture. Now many people were more interested in watching the likes of Notre Dame and Michigan on the new-fangled screen than they were in venturing out to cheer on the locals.

For 4 years, sixty years ago, WNY had its heyday of college football. It ended just about as swiftly as it had begun. But while it lasted, the sports community of WNY embraced it, the fans turned out in impressive numbers, and, of course, the players were nourished with the stuff of nostalgia. Decades later, octogenarians could reminisce fondly about the "good ol' days" of the late 1940s. Rightly so.

## CANISIUS FOOTBALL SQUAD

*1948 Great Lakes Bowl Team*

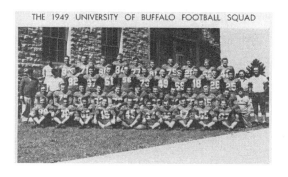

*1949 University Of Buffalo Football Team*

# Chapter 8. Sports Legacies

*Kids have always played sports. Baseball, "America's favorite pastime", was played in the streets and on sandlots in pre Little League America. Fans followed their heroes into museums and Halls of Fame. Meanwhile sports such as rowing (WSRC) became an integral part of the Buffalo sports scene.*

## Happy Birthday - WSRC
Originally printed August 2012

*For a century, the West Side Rowing Club has been a fixture on the Niagara River, a vital part of Buffalo's sports history. Many renowned Buffalonians have rowed there. A number of important regattas have taken place there. It has become one of Buffalo's most famous landmarks.*

100 years old – the West Side Rowing Club. Some think the WSRC began when Bill Cotter, born in a shell, was, like Moses found floating in the tall grass and thrushes along the Niagara River near the Black Rock Channel. Almost true! Cotter and the WSRC have been synonymous for over half a century. The 82-year-old legend is now ready to preside at the centennial celebration.

This column does NOT purport to be a centennial history of the WSRC. It is more anecdotal with personal reminiscences. However, considerable research went into my book, The Golden Age of Buffalo Sports, 1945-1950. The WSRC shone in that golden age. The Westsiders won three Royal Canadian

Henleys and dominated their Annual Labor Day regattas. The blockbuster event in that period came in July 1949 when the 75th annual Regatta of the National Association of Amateur Oarsmen was held in the Black Rock Channel. Buffalo became the rowing capital of the nation; some 350 of the country's best oarsmen participated. The local media was fulsome in its coverage and enthusiastic in its commentary. The hometown rowers captured the regatta's coveted team award as some 15,000 (that's correct, 15,000) wildly cheering spectators looked on.

My own introduction to the WSRC came in the mid-1960s. One of my neighbors was Bob Uhl. At times, I noticed that Bob seemed to vanish for weekends. I learned that he often joined Bill Cotter and other WSRC members to perform all sorts of jobs that enabled the club to operate within budget.

A few years later, while sitting in my Athletic Director's office, I caught a glimpse of a rather casual looking chap (old timers might say he resembled Perry Como) leaning over the counter in the outer office, chatting with the secretaries. I inquired as to his purpose in life and he said he was my rowing coach. That is how I met the legendary Charlie Fontana. So we had a crew. At that time, all crews were club sports. The NCAA did not recognize rowing as an NCAA sport.

A little aside: I asked Commissioner of the Eastern College Athletic Conference, Clayt Chapman why crew was not an NCAA sport. He, more or less, responded that there did not seem to be any need for that; and that the members of the Intercollegiate Rowing Association were perfectly capable of managing their own affairs. Incidentally, Chapman, a veteran of Cornell's crews was also the big gun who ran the annual ECAC regattas on Onondaga Lake at Syracuse. Navy, Wisconsin, and the Ivies joined the Orangemen as main participants; it was a big time event. I recall driving with fellow Canisius students, Klu and Shoes, to the regatta. I am not sure if the kegs of beer lining the shoreline or the races on the lake were the greater attraction. I vaguely recall seeing some guys rowing way out on the lake.

Back to Charlie Fontana – he loved coaching and he loved the rowers. His enthusiasm was so infectious that it impelled the athletic department to organize a special regatta – Canisius vs. Buff State. We marshaled our few resources – arranged for grills, food (Sahlen hot dogs of course) drinks, signage, posters all the publicity we could muster around campus and beyond and it worked. Hundreds, perhaps a thousand, turned out for the regatta off Bird Island. It was a heck of a good time. Charlie and his troops felt honored.

Charlie died suddenly in 1982, a loss for all he touched. Fortunately, his wife, Marie and his children carried on. The new Frank Lloyd Wright Boathouse, courtesy of son Tom, perpetuates the Fontana name. Daughter, Sr. Charlene, continuous to help out at regattas and serves as unofficial spiritual advisor.

In subsequent decades, the Canisius coaching duties were handled by experienced Westsiders including Jim Schaab and Jim Wynne of the legendary 1956 Melbourne Olympic crew that also featured Jim McMullen, Ron Cardwell, and Doug Turner. Other times the coaching was done by ex-Canisius rowers who honed their skills by simply being "around" the WSRC. This colorful, energetic group included: Marty Agius, Rich Schaus, (there were always Schaus's involved in Canisius Athletics), Ken Gibbons, Bill Covelli, Angelo Buscemi, Paul Kolkmeyer, and Bill Long.

Women also made their mark in rowing. Title IX was slow in catching on, but Ann Bukowski and Sue Dowd led the way with Mary Robertson and Molly Starr helping out. Wendy Bowers and Gretchen Eberl, topnotch rowers followed. The coed whom I recall as exceptional was Julie Renda. She went all out in promoting the sport at Canisius and making it work.

I have a special fondness in my athletic director's memory for those Canisius College rowers. They were truly admirable amateurs. They were undaunted, intrepid athletes – rolling out of bed on chilly spring mornings about 5:30, heading down the waterfront (when would that damn ice melt?) putting in a couple hours of tough practice and then returning for classes just about the time other students were rolling out of the sack. I don't think I ever experienced such genuine amateur athletes. They were the kind that the NCAA pretends to represent in its constitution – you know student athletes whose primary purpose is education and all that hogwash. Well you did not find those on Pac 10 football teams. But you did see them on college crews.

The college rowers asked for little (and got little). They traveled in vans, ate at roadside diners, slept on boathouse floors or in flea bitten cheap hotels. Marty Agius recalls that when his crew went to the MET Championships (which they won) they stayed at the Larchmont Motor Inn, perhaps only a tiny step above the old seamen's flophouse on Lower Main Street (Buffalo – 1940s). Marty also notes that "the best memory I have outside of rowing for Charlie Fontana was when I was coaching and had no money to pay for vans. Charlie advised me to charge it to the school, plead ignorance, and ask for forgiveness.

It worked like a charm and you (me) were a real sport about it." I think Charlie Fontana was entitled to a $200 "salary" – I don't recall that he even took that – Charlie was not exactly overpaid.

Often the Griffin crews were quite competitive. Among highlights were the trophies awarded for victories at the Dad Vail on the Schuylkill in Philadelphia and the Metropolitan Championship at New Rochelle.

Crew was good for Canisius College. Canisius played a part in the WSRC's history and there is something very special about sharing the 100th anniversary of Buffalo's esteemed Westside institution.

*The old West Side Rowing Club Boathouse that burned to the ground in 1976*

*The New Fontana Boathouse at the WSRC – a Frank Lloyd Wright Design*

*Welcome sign for the Wrightian New Fontana Boat House*

# Sports Museums – The Local Scene
Originally printed April 2013

*Museums come in all shapes and sizes. Many sport "guys" have personal collections of their favorite items. No one, at least locally, can top the collection of John Boutet. His house on Grand Island is just that – a Sports Museum.*

Now – and bigger than ever - sports museums (that often include halls of fame) are popular. The premier sports museum, without question, is Cooperstown. (Appropriately so - since baseball was the National Pastime.) Baseball authority Jim Burke feels that the meticulously arranged exhibits, e.g. Casey Stengel's, are a major reason for Cooperstown's preeminence. Dave Dengler is awed by the nearly sacred aura that envelopes the museum: players are enshrined, the plaques of the immortals are hung in a virtual sanctuary, gloves, baseball, bats, are displayed as relics. When you walk into the galley of the immortals, there is a reverence of silence; you simply do not want to talk above a whisper. In the secular world, the only place where one might stand more in awe would be before the 16th president in the Lincoln Memorial in Washington. That is truly profound.

The halls/museums for hockey (Toronto), basketball (Springfield) and football (Canton) are also first class. There are many more – Soccer, bowling, lacrosse, tennis, golf - there is a Boxing museum in Canastota, NY, home of welterweight champion, Carmen Basilio.

Individuals have their own mini museums. Stosh, from Lackawanna, attends a Bills Super Bowl loss, saves the ticket stub and begins his mini museum. A Chicago Cub fanatic (J. Maddock!) snares an Ernie Banks Homerun ball and immediately begins his collection. Todd Hannel and Mike Noga develop love affairs with the Baltimore Orioles and soon each has a space at home to savor Oriole treasures. John Hurley, Canisius President and diehard Red Sox fan has a room full of mementoes including a painting of his father in law, Danny O'Connell, a former NY Giant baseball player. Obviously, wife, Maureen is an equal partner. The Hurley's mini museum includes autographed baseballs (Ted Williams, Warren Spahn), a Gil Perrrault hockey puck, and a Muhammad Ali autographed boxing glove.

Erik Brady, premier USA Today sportswriter and a great St. Louis Cardinal fan began his collecting efforts with pink flamingos. Many may have been borrowed from lawns in Cheektowaga. Stu Boeckel, a regular at all Bison games, has his bedroom well stocked with local pro team items, as well as keepsakes from Buffalo State, Notre Dame and the Detroit Tigers.

Even I, once, thought of getting into the act. Back, circa 1944, I planned to start my collection with an 8 x 10 photo of "Shovels" Kobesky, Buffalo Bison outfielder. Shovels hit two homeruns out of Offermann Stadium the day I attended with my Dad, but it was downhill after that. The Bisons shoveled "Shovels" off to Williamsport and then into oblivion. My collection ended as quickly as it had begun.

Then there is John Boutet. Locally he reigns supreme. John's incredible collection of sports memorabilia earns the title "Sports Museum". It takes up a substantial part of his home on Grand Island so much so that Pete Calieri claims that John sleeps on the stove and his wife on the refrigerator.

The Boutet museum includes thousands of programs, ticket stubs and pennants, along with countless game-used jerseys and considerable sports equipment. Occasionally part of the Boutet collection is exhibited at Coca Cola Field, the Bison baseball stadium.

His favorite items include his own dad's 1950 Duke Snider glove, and an unused ticket from the very first Sabre's home game (vs. Montreal) - the only one known to exist.

John has the initial contract of Coach Jack Ramsay with the Braves, a Joe DeLamielleure 1970s used game helmet signed by him, OJ and Joe Fergy, Gil Perrault's first Sabre stick signed by the French Connection, a 1920's Baseball Bison wool jersey, seats from the AUD, the Rockpile, and Offermann Stadium, a turnstile from War Memorial, a 1920's All Americans football jersey, and programs from the 1879 Buffalo Baseball Bisons – that is correct, 1879.

Boutet would love (I would too) to see his treasures become part of the initial collection of a canal side museum on Buffalo's waterfront, making it, in his words, "the best this side of Cooperstown." It would certainly be far superior to the ill-fated Bass Pro Museum.

There is so much more at the Boutet museum, so much that this column just can't handle. Check out his website: www.buffalosportsmuseum.com. You will be overwhelmed.

*John Boutet, Sports Museum Head, with Legendary Bills announcer, Van Miller, and friend*

## Halls of Fame – Thousands of them
Originally printed November 2011

*Halls of fame honoring people for all sorts of achievements have become commonplace. Among the most cherished are the Athletic Halls; honoring the likes of baseball, hockey, football, basketball, soccer, boxing, and more. In Buffalo, there are several halls, the most prestigious of which is the Greater Buffalo Sports Hall of Fame.*

It's that time again – time for Halls of Fame. Usually they occur in autumn; they come in all shapes and sizes. There are walls of fame, and walks of fame, and ceilings, and floors, and who knows what else, but mostly halls. Some are downright silly; most are pretty good. The basic concept behind a HOF is admirable: honoring someone for a noteworthy achievement.

Most HOFs are of fairly recent origin, though some claim that there was a hog calling hall of fame back in colonial days. It was held in Straw Junction, Arkansas and 7 of the first 10 inductees were named Bubba. Others claim that the real first HOF was for corrupt politicians. It was started by Boss Tweed but is now defunct due to overcrowding.

There are several aviation HOFs, kind of a sign of the times. In fact, there is a robot HOF. There are also many music HOFs. We have all heard of Cleveland's Rock and Roll HOF but how about the Polka HOF? There is a burlesque hall of fame (How to qualify – Better yet- How to get named to the selection committee?).

Most HOFs focus on sports. Baseball set the standard. When the Baseball Hall of Fame was inaugurated in 1939 at Cooperstown, Ruth and Cobb led the way; the entire sports and entertainment world took notice. Baseball was without question the preeminent sport in the nation. It was, indeed, America's pastime.

The ceremonies at Cooperstown bordered on the solemn; they were inspiring. To use a favorite word of the modern generation, they were AWESOME. Ben Rader describes the Baseball Hall of Fame and Museum in quasi-religious terms. He notes that annually Americans by the thousands make the "pilgrimage" to the "shrine "at Cooperstown. There they view venerable objects: statues of larger than life heroes, "relics" including well-worn gloves, stained baseballs, soiled uniforms, and tarnished bats. Cooperstown is rich in religious terminology, "shrine"; "pantheon", "sanctuary" are used. Each year sports writers select the best for "enshrinement" after which they become "immortals." One is reminded of viewing the stained glass windows in the Chartres Cathedral or Monet's paintings in the Rouen Cathedral. The ceremonies might be likened to the canonizing of a saint in the Vatican. BUT – there is also a bit of levity. The classic (perhaps "immortal") Abbot and Costello "Who's On First?" is exhibited. To be nominated by the very selective selection committee is almost as difficult as it is for the Bills to win the Super Bowl. To use the words of Slugger Costello, the legendary peanut vender for the Elmira Pioneers, no "ham and eggers" are able to sneak in.

Pro football's Hall is equally "awesome." Upon entering the Canton HOF, the grandeur of the past puts you in a time warp. The exhibits are striking, the displays are well done; visitors are given a memorable experience. A fierce looking Dick Butkus instills fear in the onlooker.

The Hockey HOF in Toronto (where else?) is also a first class operation. It includes hands on "stuff" for the younger set. The basketball HOF in Springfield, Massachusetts is not far behind.

There are many other HOFs but most do not have the funds to acquire all the artifacts necessary for a top-notch museum.

There is a boxing HOF in central New York, featuring the likes of Carmen Basilio (the onion farmer turned middleweight champion), who lived nearby. Muhammed Ali's museum in Louisville is more comprehensive. There is a bowling HOF in St Louis; pins, balls and exotic bowling shirts are in abundance (someone thought they saw some old Blatz and Bud beer bottles and discarded packs of Old Gold cigarettes), and a soccer HOF in Oneonta, NY, once a hotbed for collegiate soccer.

Western New York has many HOFs. Most local colleges and high schools have one. Sometimes they are more inclusive – honoring persons from various fields of endeavor. Thus a 350 pound semi-literate gridiron galoot might be inducted alongside a Harvard educated molecular biologist. Ring 44 in Buffalo has an annual HOF ceremony, as does baseball. Bob Miske and Don Colpoys make sure that the annual diamond event is a rousing success.

Most HOFs have involved men. The "after 50 crowd" will recall that "back then", most females were housewives, others became nurses, teachers, or telephone operators; not much else was available. Fortunately, the past few decades have seen dramatic changes. More women are now being honored in HOFs, some for athletics; some work related; some for both, e.g. Joanne York, the triathlon champion from Mary Kay Cosmetics.

The premier local HOF is the GBSHOF, the Greater Buffalo Sports Hall of Fame. A few key people make the annual event a grandiose occasion. Among them are President Brian Cavanaugh, Teresa Forton, John Maddock, and Denny Lynch. Each year a Bill and a Sabre are selected, for obvious reasons. The other inductees vary –they might include administrators, coaches, and media types, from any level or kind of sport (the popular as well as the esoteric). The ceremonies are held in an upscale venue, excellent video presentations precede the actual induction and the responses of the honorees. President Brian Cavanaugh skillfully orchestrates the entire program. Overall the GBSHOF is simply a first class affair.

# Baseball – in the Good Ol' Days
Originally printed April 2016

*The Baseball season is here. Once again, Jim Burke and Bob Miske begin to enjoy life. Once again, they and the 60 plus age group can reflect on the Post World War II years when baseball was truly the national pastime.*

Baseball dominated the sports pages in the "old" days. No more. Today the NFL reigns supreme. Besides, there are a bewildering number of sports that compete for media attention and fan support. In no particular order: college football and basketball, NBA, NHL, auto racing and on and on. High school sports, youth sports, children sports, are all over the land. Golf is right up there. There are guys who sit glued to the Golf Channel from Thursday through Sunday year round, underscoring that specific seasons are virtually a thing of the past. Take pro football, the Super Bowl is played in February and shortly thereafter some idiotic gimmick called the Combine occurs.

Don't we remember the Combine as a piece of farm machinery?

Ah, but for those of us past 60 - there was a time when baseball was king. In fact, in the Civil War Era, around the time when Abner Doubleday did NOT invent baseball, the game soon came to be recognized as America's pastime; it remained so for over a century. Most of us may recall fondly our fathers taking us to our first baseball game. A trip to Offermann Stadium was a rite of passage. I thought I saw guys drinking "milk". I asked my Dad: "What gives?" He informed me that was beer in those cups; I was just seeing the white suds on top. Another time we stopped in a saloon on Ferry Street and Dad bought me a beer, okay a Birch beer. Just perfect!

You all remember Opening Day! What a festive occasion! It fell on a school day so you had to play hooky. "Shoes" Bewick told Sr. Helena his grand-mother died. Then he told her that three years in a row – and she wised up and Shoes got a wrap on the knuckles, plus!

But what about playing the game! Yes, every red bloodied American kid played baseball in some fashion back then, hardball it was called. Most of my friends do not recall any little leagues in those days. True there were American Legion and MUNY teams. They were for the elite ball players, a distinct minori-ty including the likes of Earle Hannel, Miske, Duggan, Jim Burke, and the Scully boys. They played organized baseball with coaches and wore slick shirts with names like Dengler Undertakers, Zuke's Saloon, or Christiano Plumbers emblazoned on the back.

The rest of us contented ourselves with playing sandlot ball. Actually, we played in the street, on a corner lot (lots of those back then), on a church lawn, and occasionally in a public park. Sometimes we used broken bats or a ball that was more like a misshapen pile of black electric tape rather than a round white object with red stitches. We loved the game; we all had the same heroes: DiMag and Ted were idolized; so too were Stan the Man, Willie "Say Hey" Mays, Jackie Robinson and Lefty Spahn.

This baseball nostalgia was brought home to me recently with the publication of "Masters of the Games" by Joel Epstein. Professor Epstein published some 25 books on literature and culture. Like another intellectual, George Will (Men at Work) Epstein has a passion for baseball; hence this work.

What is so captivating about the Epstein book is that you read a page or two and say to yourself, "Wow I remember; it was just like that," or you think "Hey that is the way we all played sports." The book brings back memories loud and clear; it is nostalgia wrapped neatly and articulately. It's like Marsh Joe McCarthy, Leo "the Lip" Durocher, the heated 1949 American League Pennant Race, and Larson's no hitter. It's a trip to Cleveland to see Bob Feller, or to Pittsburgh to see Ralph Kiner. It's listening to Bobby Thompson's historic pennant winning homerun (according to a NY Times column 50 years later, some 800,000 fans claimed to have been there in that stadium that held about 50,000). It is also Luke Easter hitting one over the centerfield scoreboard in Offermann, (vividly captured in poem by Dave Greenman). And it is also playing in the street, lining a foul ball through Mr. Parker's window, smashing it to smithereens and then hiding behind hedges (as if Parker did not know who did it). The book perfectly portrays childhood and the days of youth in the good ol' summertime.

Epstein also shares his wonderful sense of humor with regard to his Jewish background. For example, he taught in the English Department at Northwestern but helped the football staff "working with Jewish wide-receivers." That left him "lots of free time for writing". He also mentions great Jewish athletes then concludes that "the Jewish Athletes Hall of Fame could probably be accommodated in a second-floor single at your local Holiday Inn." He loved the Cubs, and Bulls, but was not much of a hockey fan, rather viewing hockey "as a secret arrangement whereby Canadians are provided with a warm place to stage fistfights." Epstein admits to not always being logical as when he roots against the Duke Basketball team because Duke had a "wretched English department filled with Marxists, deconstructionists, and other assorted goofies."

He waxes eloquently when he talks about kids play, noting today kids have all sorts of gadgets, smart phones etc. In our youth we had "a toy much less expensive and vastly more educational. The toy was called the out-of-doors."

Our generation was born before play was hyper-organized. (leagues, trophies for everyone. adult coaches, and parents totally involved). Kids organized sports themselves. Parents were rarely present; Epstein recalls one exception- one kid's father was at several games and all the other kids asked: "why the hell wasn't he working like the rest of our fathers?"

### Addendum

For me that unforgettable baseball era began when I saw Shovels Kobesky clout a homer over the right field wall in Offermann stadium (1944), landing on a porch on Woodlawn Avenue

It ended in September 1961, with the famous Mantle-Maris home run race. I was staying with my brother in his walk-up in the Bronx just off the Grand Concourse, less than a mile from Yankee stadium. My brother was a great Yankee fan and we thrilled to the Mantle-Maris homerun race, happening, literally, just down the street. What a great end to a fabulous era.

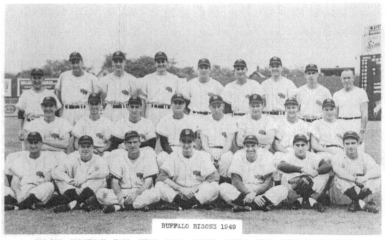

BUFFALO BISONS 1949

TOP ROW: PEPPERDAY, WADE, OKRIE, ALOMA, HOOPER, HARRIS, BYAM, TRECHOCK, CORCORAN
MIDDLE ROW: TRIPLETT, DeMARS, ROGOVIN, RICHARDS, CRAMER, MOORE, FREY, COLEMAN
BOTTOM ROW: HAUSMANN, MARKLAND, WARREN, PARTON, BLOCK, SILVERMAN, TABACHECK

*Buffalo Bisons 1949 Baseball Team, International League Champs*

*Home of the Buffalo Bisons - 1935-1960*

*All-time great Yankee manager, Joe McCarthy. Joe lived at Gates Circle and later on Ellicott Creek farm*

*Paul Richards – Bison Champion Manager 1949. Richards was the all-star catcher for the World Series Champions – Detroit Tigers in 1945*

# Little Leagues Have Changed
Originally printed June 2011

*In the decade after WWII, only top shelf athletic kids played organized baseball.*
*But baseball was America's pastime; everyone played at least sandlot baseball. Then came the*
*phenomenal growth of little league baseball and just about anyone who wanted, played on some*
*sort of organized team replete with team jersey and cap.*

Ten-year-old Nick Hassett and his big brother, Joey, appeared in sparkling new tee shirts proudly proclaiming that the North Buffalo Little League
(Shoshone variety) was established in 1954. That was it. That confirmed for me
that little leagues were not around when I was a youngster in the 1940s. Once
"little league" meant baseball, now it covers many sports. In recent decades little
league has come to mean that kids, boys and girls, of varying athletic skills (or
none), are able to participate in sports of their choosing. That is simply great.
All kids should have that opportunity. If they lose, and lose constantly, so be
it, that is part of life. "They" say that that teaches something or other, just as
winning teaches something too.

I suggested the little league topic at our Tuesday night roundtable at the
Wellington Pub; vigorous discussion ensued. But in a gentlemanly way we
reached agreement, no guns blazed, no knives brandished, no harsh vulgarities
uttered (to the amazement of a later generation).

We focused on the decade after WWII. It was agreed that then only good
players participated in any sort of organized baseball. John Christiano and Jim
Burke were pretty fair players – so they played on organized teams. I was absolutely horrible, plus wore glasses and was tagged "four eyes" in those pre-politi-
cally correct days. I wonder if that stunted my psychological growth; they forgot
to tell me. Andy Moynihan grew up in Wisconsin knowing all about cheese and
Packer football, later he was a St Joes baseball standout. Bob Dickerson played
in the Albany area later, some say while dodging freight trains (his first love).
Henry Kaye was an excellent player for Canisius College, and Paul Reister had
baseball in his blood, supervising the parochial school leagues, seemingly forever.

We then reminisced about diamond standouts whose names appeared
occasionally on the Courier's sport pages. In fact, a new book on Warren
Spahn – the greatest to ever play baseball here, mentioned that Spahn grew up

in Kaisertown, and played on midget and American Legion teams. He was the best, but there were many other very good ones: including George Daddario, Ken Fremming, Bobby Miske and Tommy Flynn. In South Buffalo - the "Caz" park guys – featured the likes of Don Colpoys, Tommy McCarthy, Tommy Van Remman, Tommy Ryan and many more. The big star over in Riverside Park was Sharkey Diebold (and my Dad, but he played way back in the 20's). The Kenmore Yankees were led by slugger Jack Duggan, the Watson boys, Joe Carver, and Bob Lee. The Fillmore-Leroy area had a magnificent pitcher, Earle Hannel and a solid second sacker, Joe Scully. Joe Bieron claims he had great potential in that same area.

Organized baseball right after the war, was primarily the midget and American Legion variety - limited to the talented 10th. The rest of us clods played sandlot ball. We played on the corner vacant lot or sometimes in the street. Here is the way it went: after school, the local kids gathered. Some guy brought a bat, another lad came up with a ball (sometimes wrapped with black electric tape). Sides were selected by wrapping your fingers round the bat, and the game began. You played for a while usually until your mom called you for dinner. Or if your game was in the street, you played until one kid drove the ball through a neighbor's window. That ended it for the day.

But just about every red-blooded American kid was a baseball fan in those days. The sport merited being labeled the National Pastime. Offermann Stadium was the mecca; locals thought it grander than Yankee Stadium, though only about one tenth the size. To sit there in the bleachers being bleached in the hot sun while your heroes were playing the Jersey City Giants was ecstasy. Those who longed to watch the Major leaguers could take a bus excursion, courtesy of Andy Moynihan enterprises, and head for Cleveland.

All of that has changed over the past half century. The city neighborhood teams and parks are pretty much antiquated, though the Shoshone and Cazenovia baseball programs still flourish. Little leagues, fortunately, have become egalitarian. Even the youngster who doesn't know the top from the bottom of the bat or the young fraulein who doesn't know the difference between a baseball bat and a croquet mallet now have a chance to participate. Athletic organizations have mushroomed. The suburbs grew tremendously in the 50's and kept growing in the decades that followed.

Moreover the concept of "little league" has broadened. It used to be restricted to baseball, now it covers some 20 sports for both sexes. Some youngsters start participating as soon as they learn to walk. Baseball itself has faded at least a little. Look at Delaware Park where there used to be four big time diamonds. Now there are two - room had to be made for soccer fields. In the suburbs, there are sprawling parks that include many athletic fields of all types. Soccer Moms and Hockey Dads are in abundance there and have been for decades. That's where the action is and it is very diverse.

*North Park Little League, slugger, Nick Hassett and ACE pitcher,*
*Joey Hassett*

# Chapter 9. War Years

*Our country's wars, especially World War II, were often topics of conversation. D-Day, VJ Day, and VE Day were remembered in various ways. Honor Flights, the GI Bill, as well as the War of 1812, and the Fenians were also of interest.*

## The War of 1812: Facts, Fiction and?

Originally printed September 2012

*A rather off beat quiz on the War of 1812 and a brief overview of that War and its significance in our area. Most Americans are blissfully ignorant about the War of 1812. Check out this quiz (previously given to local yokels) to see how you rate.*

### Quiz:

1. When did the War of 1812 take place? WOW – talk about being up on the news: 92% knew the answer. 8% - not sure.

2. Who were the main opponents in the war? 40% correctly said - the US vs Great Britain; 26% between France and Russia noting that "everyone knows" that Tchaikovsky's 1812 overture commemorates Napoleon's retreat from Moscow.

3. In 1813 British troops crossed the Niagara and burned the tiny village of Buffalo. Why? 25% said the Brits wanted to clean up the East side around the Broadway Market. 43% said it was part of Mayor Jimmy

Griffin's urban renewal program. Correct: Historian Frank Eberl notes that the British landed at Black Rock (appropriate markers now abound in the area) and torched Buffalo in retaliation for the Americans burning York (Toronto).

4. Name two famous commanders on the Niagara Frontier: 67% said General Patton, 2% said Colonel Sanders. Correct: Scott (US), Brock (Brit.) Scott used the Banigan home in Williamsville for winter headquarters; later a Mexican War hero.

5. Identify the Battle of Lake Erie. 23% said it was a Buffalo Bills victory over the Cleveland Browns though 10% of those said neither could really win a football game! 45% said it involved 2 Russian nuclear subs, 43 Navy Seals, and a tugboat from the Buffalo harbor. Correct: Capt. Perry of US won, Sept. 1813.

6. Complete the famous saying of that Battle: "Don't give up the _____"
   a)40 kegs of Genesee Beer b) Plans for a 2nd Peace Bridge – Correct: SHIP

7. Identify Lundy's Lane: 76% recognized it was famous for cheap motels and strip joints; 10% recognized it from a sign on the QEW. Correct answer: one of the bloodiest battles of the entire war, ending pretty much in a draw.

8. Identify the Battle of Newark? Most said it was fought in New Jersey in the 1960s. Correct: Newark is now Niagara on the Lake and according to Kevin Greenwald was the scene of unnecessary bloodshed of civilians in Dec. 1813.

9. Identify the Battle of Chippawa: 55% said it was fought outside the 67 bars on Chippewa in downtown Buffalo. Correct: another bloody engagement fought about 30 Kilometers south of Lundy's Lane.

10. Here is an easy one: Identify Fort Erie: 45% said it was a fort built during Prohibition to facilitate the shipping of booze to Buffalo. 20% said Eliot Ness used it as a base to machine gun the rum runners headed for the 1st Ward. 30% said that Ft. Erie was a town composed of 93 Chinese restaurants and several Canadian ballets. Correct: An actual fort

that Americans captured then abandoned near the end of the war.

Quiz winners: those who scored in the highest percentile will be given a free tour of Black Rock with local authority Frank Eberl as tour guide.

## Some straight facts - especially pertaining to the Niagara Frontier:

The war commenced June 1812. Causes included: affronts to American's honor by the British Navy on the high seas; American thirst for Western Expansion and suspicions that Britain was encouraging Tecumseh and his Indians to resist Americans.

Early battles – at Queenston Heights and Crysler's Farm; embarrassing defeats for those Americans who thought it would be easy to conquer some of Brit Canada.

The infant Navy won some glorious victories on the high seas, e.g. US Constitution (Old Ironsides).

Military historian, Colonel Bob Dickerson, notes that 1814 saw the bloodiest fighting of the war, and it took place along the Niagara. On July 3rd, General Scott led the army (he had trained them well in Williamsville) to capture Fort Erie. A few days later they were victorious over the Brits and their Indian allies at Chippawa. On July 25th the bloody battle of Lundy's Lane was fought. It ended in pretty much a draw with heavy casualties (hundreds killed) on both sides.

American forces drew back to Fort Erie. British attacked in mid-August but without success. As the war drew to a close US troops withdrew from Fort Erie to Buffalo figuring they no longer needed the Fort.

Meanwhile in 1813-14, about 32 kilometers (20 miles) due west of Fort Erie along the Lake Erie Canadian shore, the Sugarloaf settlement played an important role in the War. The area was sparsely populated with a mixture of Mennonites and Quakers (emigrated there in the 1700s) as well as the Sherk clan (Sherkston Quarry, Sherk Lumber) and Loyalists who fled America following the Revolution.

Loaf historian Dr. Dick Munschauer notes that Sugarloaf Hill is the most prominent elevation (100 meters?) on the Canadian shore. It served as a guide-post for ships and troop movements. Nearby at Gravelly Bay was the Zavitz Mill, vital for provisions, especially flour. American raiders ransacked the area for provisions: the Quakers and Mennonites (though pacifists) supplied needed food for the British troops and Canadian volunteers. Today Sugarloaf hill continues to be an important landmark and the Marsh/Sugarloaf Farm at its base a popular resort.

**Postscript:**

American history textbooks are woefully inadequate on the War of 1812. Fortunately, efforts are underway to increase our awareness of the war. A number of books and pamphlets have been published about the conflict and the bicentennial celebrations. Local TV, the Buffalo News, the Buffalo/Erie County Historical Society and the Canadian media have provided special programs and stories. Western New York Heritage Magazine (Editor Doug DeCroix is an expert on the war) is featuring a 3-part series on the war beginning this fall. Mike and Charity Vogel have made us aware of major events in the Buffalo Harbor area, September 11th-18th. The legendary brig, the Niagara, will dock there. The Naval Park (Colonel Pat Cunningham, assisted by Colonel Jim McNicholas) features a superb mapped chronology of the war highlighting the Niagara Frontier. A new visitors' center at Fort Erie recently opened. The Niagara Falls (Ontario) Historical Museum features a new gallery which highlights the War on the Canadian/Niagara frontier. The Port Colborne Maritime Museum has impressive material on the Sugarloaf area.

*War of 1812 plaque marking the site of skirmishes in Black Rock*

*Fenian plaque: Erected on 150th Anniversary of Fenian-Irish raid on Canada at Black Rock Park*

# The Fenians: Irish Warriors
Originally printed October 2016

*The Fenians, (Irish Americans of Buffalo), tried to attack England via Canada. They embarked from Black Rock, in 1866, crossed the Niagara, fought their way to Ridgeway, then backtracked to the First Ward, ever after to be occasionally celebrated for their indomitable spirit.*

The Fenians! Who? So you do not know much about the history of the Fenians? Don't feel bad. Some students think World War II came before World War I. The local Fenians just celebrated the 150th anniversary of the legendary Fenian Raid.

I refer to a Buffalo group of disgruntled, patriotic Irish Americans of the 1860s who wanted to do their part to free Ireland from British control. These Irish freedom fighters thought that they could accomplish their aim by "twisting the Lions (British) tail". Thus, if they invaded Canada, which was then part of the British Empire, they could put pressure on Great Britain to move toward granting Irish independence.

These spirited Fenians left the First Ward and gathered at Black Rock on the Niagara River.

Many Fenians had emigrated from Ireland during the famine. Some were seasoned soldiers, veterans just a year removed from combat experience during the recent American Civil War.

They crossed the Niagara River and battled their way to Ridgeway. Their success was fleeting. British troops began arriving in very large numbers; they came from Toronto. The Fenians fell back to Fort Erie. No assistance was forthcoming from the American government. The Irish firebrands had to hang their heads in ignominy and head back to American soil.

But the Fenians did carve out for themselves a heroic and colorful page in our history.

In 1966, on the 100th anniversary of the Fenian Raid some local Irish Americans decided to reenact the raid. Fueled with good intentions and good Guinness, they embarked in motor boats from Black Rock and landed in Fort Erie. Congressman Max McCarthy and legendary singer J. B. Walsh provided leadership. They met with men from the 10th Field Artillery Regiment, a military unit that had been formed as a result of the original Fenian Raid. Both sides joined in some conviviality.

This past May, the 150th anniversary of the raid was celebrated with a gala parade in Ridgeway, Ontario. In Buffalo the sesquicentennial celebration took place at the foot of Hertel Avenue where a plaque marks the original embarkation site. There the renowned Irish Historian Ed Patton delivered remarks that spoke eloquently of the place of the Fenians in local history as well as the significance that the Fenians had on later Irish history.

The abortive Easter Rebellion of 1916 owes something to the inspiration of the original Fenians as does the Civil War that took place between the Irish and the Brits in the 1920s; the conflict that did result in the Irish gaining their independence.

Irish Americans in Buffalo and elsewhere continue to celebrate all things Irish, often on a moment's notice. The Commemoration at the Irish Famine monument near the Harbor is proclaimed widely by Mike (the "Carnation Lad") Flynn, as well as by Kathleen Delaney and Bob Farrington. The latter claims an ancestral bond with all Kennedys in Limerick. Tim Bohen of the prolific Bohen clan and the inestimable Ed Patton.as well as Kevin Townsell, producer of the annual mammoth Irish Festival, are Irish types to be reckoned with.

The Fenian spirit lives on. In fact just recently a new restaurant, the Tewksbury Lodge opened in the First Ward on the river directly across from the Labatts Blue silos. It is operated by prominent Ward resident, Peg Overdorf. One of the eye-catching menu items is: The Fenian.

Back in the latter decades of the 19th century, it might be said that the Fenian cause was partially successful. I refer to the fact, verified by Canadian Shore historian Joe Bieron, that some Americans bought prime real estate all along the Lake Erie shore from Erie Beach to Point Abino. They successfully "invaded" Canada. It was a peaceful invasion. Not many Irish were involved. It was primarily the work of wealthy WASPS from Buffalo, who had made fortunes in the rising commerce and industry in Buffalo in the closing decades of the 19th century. One plutocrat would buy extensive acreage, (hectares) and then sell off parcels to his friends and family. Bieron further notes that the rising middle class waited until the World War II era to stake their claims to cottage areas on the Canadian shore further west. Of course, once again, the tide is turning, at least a little. In the early 21st century, Canadians, especially from the Toronto area, are purchasing land along Canada's Cote d'Azur? What goes around comes around!

# June 6, 1944 - D - DAY
Originally printed June 2012

*Some of us still remember D Day, June 6, 1944. It filled our young minds with great anticipation. It is a date always remembered but in recent decades even more so. The local connection, with the Niland boys, and the film, Saving Private Ryan, has given D Day special meaning for Western New Yorkers.*

It was a sunny June morning, a long time ago - as usual I left for school about 8: am. But, not as usual, my mom excitedly announced that it was D-Day. Off to school I went, meeting Jack Duggan on the way. We crossed at Elmwood: Jimmy the policeman was there. I asked him about D-Day; negative, he had not yet heard the morning news. When I arrived home that afternoon, Mom, who it seemed followed the progress of WWII as closely as Winston Churchill, filled me in with the latest news reports.

Being only 10 and hardly a child prodigy, I did not think much more about D-Day at the time. Over the years, that changed. In fact, for most Americans, it seemed that a big change came in 1984, the 40th anniversary, when President Reagan went to Normandy. The Great Communicator delivered, as the Associate Press stated: "one of the great performances of his life." He stood near the Pointe du Hoc. Old soldiers wept and millions watched TV in silence, as the President poignantly described how the Army Rangers had scaled the cliffs facing almost certain death. D-Day began the long arduous task of bringing the war to an end. WWII was acknowledged as the watershed event of the 20th century and D-Day came to receive the attention that it was due. Books, films, and television specials, began to be produced in record numbers.

Back at St Paul's School during the war years, 6th grade teacher, Sr. Marie Thomas, aka Frances Niland, said to some of us: "You boys who love basketball should know about my brothers, Tommy and Joe Niland, they were All Americans." Indeed they were; they played for Canisius when the Golden Griffins had a national reputation. That is how I first learned about the Nilands. Joe became the legendary basketball coach of Canisius College in the late 1940s. In the 1970s when I was Director of Athletics, Joe returned to help out as an assistant coach. As AD, I attended many athletic meetings where I came to know Tommy Niland, then AD at LeMoyne College. I would listen to him talk, at great length, about the war. Tom was a paratrooper – wounded at the Battle of the Bulge.

His brother, whom he referred to as Tanker Joe, was with Patton's Third Army.

My involvement with the Nilands increased as did my interest in WWII. Some years later I hired a Niland nephew, John Beilein, (presently at Michigan) as head basketball coach at Canisius. In fact when I hired him, I received a humorous note from Sr. Marie Thomas saying "Danny, you finally did something right." Another Niland, David, became one of John's assistants. David is now the successful head coach at Penn State Behrend.

In 1998, the highly acclaimed Steven Spielberg film, Saving Private Ryan, was released. One of the best WWII films ever, it was based in part on the four Niland boys of the Michael Niland branch of the family, cousins of Joe and Tom. The DVD that I used often in my American history classes featured an epilogue, in which Tom Hanks and Spielberg discussed the making of the film, the role of the Nilands, and interviews with family members. Of the four Nilands, two died in the Normandy invasion, Robert and Preston. A third, Edward, had been reported missing in action in Burma (sometime later they found that he had survived a Japanese Prisoner of War camp), and the fourth, Fritz (Pvt. Ryan), parachuted in at Normandy, and was located a few days later by a chaplain, and returned to stateside duty.

In the years that followed I often kibitzed with various Nilands, especially Joe and Tom, about World War II and D-Day. David, Joe's son, told me that when he was young his Dad often talked to him about the war. Pictures of the D-Day Nilands adorned the mantle at their home. The Nilands were a close knit family; in fact the extended Niland family became legendary in Tonawanda. Before the war all the boys were star athletes at Tonawanda High School. Preston went to UB, all the others attended Canisius College. God, Country, Family - the Nilands (male and female) embraced that adage completely. Indeed, if women could have served in combat, Sr. Marie Thomas would have been a Ranger. Legend had it that in the 1970s, when she was serving at St Mary of Sorrows, in a rather bleak part of Buffalo, a burglar entered her bedroom, grabbed her purse and fled. She awoke, chased him down Genesee Street (to the astonishment of neighbors) and tackled him. That was mostly true according to Martha Lamparelli (Niland). The thief was chased – but rather than risk being pummeled by a nun, he dropped the purse and vanished into the night. Yes, the Nilands were tough. Joe did not get the nickname "Piler Joe" for nothing. If there was a football pile-up, Joe would be in the middle of it.

Last October, my wife and I visited Normandy: the cliffs, beaches, gun emplacements, the impressive new visitor center (opened 2007) and the cemetery. The visitor center with its magnificent displays - photographs, film clips, memorabilia, and documents - offered a comprehensive visual and audio history of D-Day events.

Just before exiting the visitor center, you pass through a picture gallery. On all four walls are hung individual photographs, perhaps 24" by 20" of significant figures involved in D-Day: statesmen and generals, as well as privates and sergeants, perhaps a total of 30. All were single photographs individually displayed with one exception. Four photographs were grouped together - a square display of four soldiers, the four Niland boys from Tonawanda. The caption appropriately noted the film, Saving Private Ryan. It was a genuinely emotional moment as I stood there recalling memories of the Nilands and thought back to the many times I showed the film to classes.

Then outside and down the lane, exactly as portrayed in the film are the beaches of Normandy stretched out on one side and the cemetery with its rows of glistening white crosses placed with geometric precision on the other. Eventually one comes to Section 15 row 4 and stops at the two crosses marking the graves of Preston and Robert Niland. (In a quiet moment of perfect silence one thinks of the huge sacrifices made by so many.)

For me it was a full cycle moment: Recalling my mom in 1944 ecstatically telling me about the invasion that she heard on the old Philco radio - and now 67 years later visiting the site of one of the most momentous military events of world history.

*Four Niland Boys, made famous in "Saving Private Ryan,"
on wall at D-Day Visitors Center*

*Remembering at D-Day Normandy Cemetery*

# VE Day/Memorial Day Celebrations
Originally printed July 2015

*Victory in World War II in Europe was celebrated widely. Parades on Memorial Day are on-going.*

Recently VE Day, Victory in Europe, was celebrated. May 8th, 1945 marked the end of World War II in Europe. Understandably it was celebrated more in Europe than America. Much of the continent was laid waste, virtually demolished by the war against Hitler and his Nazis. Rick Atkinson's masterful trilogy on World War II in Europe gives us an idea of the extensive devastation caused by the conflict and an understanding why WWII is considered the most cataclysmic event in world history. There are thousands of books written about the war, Atkinson's are among the very best.

Victory in Europe was expected, anticipated. The Allies pretty much knew that Germany's defeat was imminent in the spring of 1945. D Day, June 6th, 1944, was labeled "the beginning of the end." After establishing a beachhead in Normandy, Allied troops broke out of the hedgerows and liberated Paris by the end of August. Then it was on to the German border. Meanwhile Russians were driving the Germans back out of Eastern Europe.

The British, Canadian, and American troops ran into a major problem, The Battle of the Bulge! That was Hitler's last ditch effort, where he threw everything, including the kitchen sink, at the Allies, temporarily halting their advance in Dec-Jan. By the end of January, 1945 the "Good Guys" were again on the march toward the Rhine. That legendary river was crossed at Remagen on March 7th. By the end of April, American and Russian troops were shaking hands at the Elbe River. The Germans were finished.

Europeans were jubilant. Celebrations in the U.S. were restrained. Japan still had to be defeated and unconditional surrender by the Japanese seemed nowhere in sight.

In fact the biggest battle of the Pacific theater was still raging. American Marines swept ashore on Okinawa on April 1st, the army joined them. Vicious battles ensued; Okinawa was not declared secure until June 22nd. A personal note, I delivered the Courier Express as a kid and was aware of the flags with stars flown in the windows of many of my customers. The Flynns had a couple of boys in the service, one never came home. Lt. James Hawkins, who lived two streets from me, was killed on Okinawa on June 10th. Lt. Leo Lyons was wounded there. Many years later Ray Manuzewski told me about his experience as a Marine corpsman (medic) on Okinawa. Wow, talk about hazardous duty. Here is the point about this segue, Ray told me that his 6th Marine Division knew that once the Okinawa battle was over, the invasion of Japan was next. I have heard this same story from countless other veterans I have interviewed over the past 3 decades. Many of the military in Europe had already prepared for the long troop ship voyage to the other side of the world to take part in the invasion of Japan.

The predictions were that Japan would have to be invaded, probably in late 1945, and the best estimates stated that Japan would probably not surrender until late 1946. The Atomic Bomb had not yet been tested. No wonder the celebrations of VE day were muted in the U.S.

Nevertheless it was good to see the many recent remembrances of World War II, of VE Day and D Day. The annual National Memorial Day Concert from the Mall in Washington was exceptional. In addition to the usual medley of military marching songs, this year's program told the stories of recent veterans who had served in Vietnam, Iraq, and Afghanistan. Highlights included heart rendering tributes to wounded and disabled vets of those conflicts.

The media, yes the much criticized media, seemed to be at its best. Local TV, The Buffalo News and the community newspapers, had a number of stories of local interest. Radio filled the airwaves with patriotic music. Channel 2's Pete Gallivan did his usual fine job especially with D Day programs tying in local connections such as the Niland Boys and the film Saving Private Ryan. Several of the World War II classic films were shown.

Finally, the Memorial Day parades! They seemed to have been around forever. Indeed some do date from the time of the Civil War; they have become part of the fabric of communities in America. Among the most enduring and popular parades have been those in Williamsville and Kenmore/Tonawanda. I have been watching the Kenmore parade, off and on, for seven decades. They have changed. At the most recent one, there were at least 5 marching bands, some veteran groups and several fire trucks accompanied by their proud marching, fully uniformed firemen and firewomen. Back in the 1940s, there were the traditional fire departments but just one marching band. Reflecting the pride of World War II there were several veteran contingents: Catholic War Veterans, Jewish War Veterans, The American Legion, Veterans of Foreign Wars among others. Taking up the rear were perhaps as many as 5000 boy scouts and a smattering of girl scouts, cubs and brownies. At the head of the scouting contingent was "Pop" Hauser. I think he was the Head of all scouts in Erie County. He was seated in a shiny convertible, kind of looking like Emperor Caesar Augustus leading the Roman Legions into Gaul. "Shoes" Bewick, the "Fringer" and myself were part of the scene, marching (helter skelter) behind scout leaders Banigan and Raiff. We were decked out in various parts of the official uniform. Some wore scout caps, others had a shirt and kerchief, some a belt; not many could afford a full scout outfit in those days. The end of the parade seemed to disintegrate; it might have been labeled complete disarray! Nonetheless cherished memories abounded.


## The A Bomb and VJ Day
Originally printed August 2015

*70 years ago, I was out at my Grandpa's farm, helping out (kind of) with farm work. It was a hot August 6th. Uncle Charlie came out of the farmhouse and said "We just dropped the Atomic Bomb?" I said, "What's that?" He said he didn't know but he thought it was something huge.*

Who did know anything about the A Bomb then? Very few! The Manhattan Project, the entity, which developed the atomic bomb, was super-secret. Could you imagine such a four year project being a secret today? Parts of the bomb were developed and manufactured all over the US, at the Univ. of Chicago; Hanover, Washington; Los Alamos, New Mexico and Oakridge, Tennessee. More than 100,000 workers were employed. And it remained top secret.

Today the news media, internet, twitter, your everyday hacker, would have followed the development of the A bomb in detail from its inception. Transparency and clarity would be demanded as a right in our democratic society. Enemy spies would, of course, be in on all the secrets. Some twit would be declaring that the A Bomb was being transported from Los Alamos to San Francisco and then arriving in Saipan at 8:23 on July 23, and then pinpointing the Hiroshima target. The secret held 70 years ago, but today??

Back to 1945! The Atomic Bomb was dropped on Hiroshima August 6, three days later the second bomb fell on Nagasaki. On August 14 President Truman announced the Japanese (Japs as the politically incorrect news services called them) surrendered.

What followed the Truman announcement was the biggest, spontaneous celebration that I, and probably anyone else in America, ever witnessed. Truly awesome!

From Times Square to San Francisco's Union Square and in every town and hamlet in between, including Buffalo's Lafayette Square, it was pandemonium. Hirohito was hung in effigy in the Kensington-Bailey section of the city, the Broadway-Fillmore intersection resembled Times Square on New Year's Eve. Betty Hughes recalls that up and down the American and Canadian shores of Lake Erie, bonfires lit up the sky. Betty was pleased that now her 6 brothers, all in the military, would be on their way home. George Wilcox heard the surrender while finishing up B-29 flight school in Texas. He was sent to Manila but happy that the invasion of Japan was now a dead issue. Jim Foley on duty aboard a destroyer escort off Okinawa was pleased too. Marine Ray Manuzewski, survived the gruesome battle of Okinawa but was not looking forward to the Marines' invasion of mainland Japan. Obviously Ray was relieved when he heard the Atomic Bomb ended the war; Ray headed for Tientsin, China.

I lived six houses from Delaware Avenue in the middle of Kenmore. I heard noise, loud noise. I rushed down to Delaware – chaos prevailed everywhere: Fire and ambulance sirens going full blast, car horns blaring, kids banging on pots and pans, and people hanging out windows waving flags, screaming and crying. The likes of Zuke, Stooch, and Tony E. emerged from the Kenmore Tavern and the Golden Pheasant, jitterbugging in the street. Joe Scully witnessed the North Park area in jubilant chaos. Church bells of all denominations rang incessantly; people filed into churches to thank the Almighty that "it" was over. The celebrations went on into the night. The American people had indeed "let loose". Never anything like it, NEVER. The following day the largest crowd in the city's history gathered on the Delaware Park Meadow for a victory celebration with Buffalo's most famous radio personality, Clint Buehlman, serving as Master of Ceremonies. (Footnote: The official Japanese surrender took place on September 2 aboard the US Missouri in Tokyo Bay).

Thank Heavens for the Necessary Atomic Bomb.

Over the past half century, I have taught, lectured, researched and written about the A Bomb. The most asked question: "Was it necessary?" Absolutely! In recent years revisionists, some well-intentioned, have contended that the A Bomb was not necessary because Japan was already on the verge of surrender.

They are dead wrong. If it were not for the A Bomb, the estimates were that the war would have gone on for at least another year, and with far more casualties than occurred in Hiroshima and Nagasaki.

As the American forces "island hopped" across the Pacific, the closer they came to Japan the higher the death tolls. On Iwo Jima, Feb. 1945, 7,000 marines were killed. On Okinawa, the closest islands to Japan, some 12,000 American lives were lost and at least 36,000 wounded. Japanese deaths totaled 110,000 and the Okinawa civilian population suffered 150,000 deaths (more than Hiroshima).

I have interviewed countless veterans of WWII over the years, and to a man they say that after they had witnessed the ruthless resistance of the Japanese soldiers, on Iwo and especially on Okinawa, they knew that Japan would have to be invaded. The costs would be staggering.

The Japanese were fierce opponents, preferring death to surrender; in fact never once during the war did a single Japanese unit surrender.

Many written accounts attest to the tenacity of the Japanese soldiers. The best in my view is E. B. Sledge's "With the Old Breed: At Peleliu and Okinawa." A classic! Many WWII authorities rate it as the best memoir on the war. Nearly as compelling and sobering is William Manchester's "Goodbye Darkness, a Marine Memoir of the Pacific War". Both give incredible personal accounts of Japanese resistance. Read about the Marines' doggedly bloody attempts to take Okinawa's Sugarloaf Hill in May, 1945 and you will get an understanding of what the invasion of Japan would have been like. The death toll would have been astronomical, much higher than Hiroshima and Nagasaki.

Yes, the bomb was horrible. No one can be happy that so many people were killed. But it was necessary to drop it. It did bring the war to a quick close. It assuredly saved many more lives than were lost at Hiroshima and Nagasaki. Truman's decision was the appropriate one. Alonzo Hamby, a Truman biographer, put it as succinctly as any authority. He concluded: "All humane individuals would prefer that the bomb had not been used. Many scholars, after careful examination of the sources, nonetheless have come to the conclusion that it was necessary."

*Times Square - VJ Day 1945, one of the most famous photos ever*

## Celebrating the GI Bill's 70th Anniversary
Originally printed October 2014

*The GI Bill (1944), for those who served in the military before 1955, was a Godsend. Sometimes called the greatest law ever passed by Congress, it enabled millions to earn a college degree.*

That law has been called one of the most successful pieces of legislation in American history. On a par with the Social Security Act of 1935 and the Land Grant Acts of the mid-19th century! Popularly known as the GI Bill, it is officially known as: "The Servicemen's Readjustment Act of 1944."

Congress (Republicans and Democrats), and the President, saw that it was imperative to avoid the catastrophe that engulfed veterans after WW I. There were 16 million men and women in uniform in WWII. With millions returning to civilian life following the war, the GI Bill, spearheaded by the American Legion, became law. Simply put: It revolutionized America.

In 1944 when the details of the program were being worked out, voices of dissent were raised. Many simply said the country could not afford the astronomical cost. James Conant, president of Harvard (whom Poet Robert Frost called "a prude and a Puritan") opposed the bill saying that the veterans would pollute higher education especially in the finest schools of the East. Interestingly enough, just a few years later, Conant and other Ivy presidents were praising vets at their institutions for raising academic standards. A Yale dean was enthusiastic about the "excellent quality" of the vets.

The essence of the bill was this: all WWII vets were entitled to cash payments for tuition and living expenses for education as well as low cost mortgages and one year of unemployment compensation (52/20 - $20 for 52 weeks). Seems amazing but only about 20 percent of the unemployment funds were utilized.

The GI Bill had its limitations. There were some scandals. I mean with billions of dollars, it was almost inevitable that some corruption and fraud would creep in. But overall, it was hugely successful. Author Edward Humes summarized the resulting benefit: it made homeowners, and college grads and a "booming middle class out of a Depression-era generation that never expected such opportunity."

In 1946, there were few signs of the silent revolution that would transform college campuses. Soon GIs started to attend in record numbers. Admissions were informal, costs were not an issue. The vets proved to be excellent students, faculty were elated. Since all expenses were covered, many veterans matriculated at the Ivy schools, colleges that earlier only the elite attended (and today they cost a fortune to attend). Harvard's enrollment almost doubled. Why go to Podunk U. when the government will send you to Yale, Time magazine asked? I recall alumni from Brown, Harvard, Colgate and Middlebury and other prestigious institutions. I thought their folks must have been well heeled. Later I learned that they were from modest background and were it not for the GI Bill they may not have graduated from those first rate institutions.

The dedicated vets wanted to "get that degree" and get on with life. But some did engage in other activities: beer-drinking (but no wearing beanies) and of course sports.

Glance at the football rosters of our local Big 4 colleges in the late 40s. UB, CC, Niagara, and Bona - each had competitive teams. They were so because they suited up many vets, who were, in effect, on full athletic (GI Bill) scholarships, equivalent to a full ride at USC. The proof is in the pudding. When the vets graduated, the local institutions could not afford the full rides and so: UB football went into remission for a few years, CC dropped it in 1950, Niagara in 1951, and Bona in 1952.

College enrollments, down during the Depression, hit all-time lows during

WWII (750,000). Even Ivies suffered, e.g. Yale in 1944, had a total undergrad enrollment of 565 in 1944; before the war the frosh class was over 800. By 1950 college enrollments were at an all-time peak. By the time the original GI Bill ended nearly 8 million of the 16 million veterans had participated in an education or training program.

Not only did the GI Bill change significantly higher education in the US but it also changed the landscape. It brought into existence modern suburbia. "It is no exaggeration to say that the creation of suburbia and extension of home ownership" to a majority of American families was "launched, underwritten, and paid for by the GI Bill" (Humes).

In the decades that followed WWII, America changed so dramatically that today's young people simply cannot imagine the world in which their grandparents or great grandparents lived in 1940.

A high percentage of families then lived in rural areas or in crowded cities. Suburbs were few. On a farm electricity and flush toilets were rare. Water came from a pump. In cities you found families of seven or eight residing in a two bedroom house with one toilet. By today's standards a large part of the population seemed poor - though they did not realize it. There was almost always food on the table and clothes (often hand-me-downs) to wear. Vacations were unheard of. A family car – rare! Only the wealthy took a morning shower; the rest took a Saturday bath.

Arthur Levitt was instrumental here. Almost overnight he changed the way homes were produced. Levitt adopted assembly line techniques. Don't build homes one at a time, build an entire neighborhood. Levitt bought a large potato farm on Long Island and almost overnight created Levittown. At one time he sold 1400 homes a day. A vet with no money down could now with his GI loan become a homeowner. Hundreds of thousands of these homes were constructed over the new few years. In Western New York, a personal example: in 1947, my Boy Scout troop from Kenmore, camped out in tents erected in the fields and woods in an area near Sheridan Drive and Niagara Falls Boulevard. Just two years later, Pearce and Pearce Homebuilders, constructed hundreds of houses on that very land, now known as Lincoln Park. Throughout the nation hundreds of "Levittowns" were constructed. The 1950s became the biggest decade of suburban growth in all of American history.

The GI Bill was a terrific investment: It cost 51 billion (in today's dollars), yet the return was some 260 billion in increased economic output for those educated GIs and another 93 billion on extra taxes paid. Seven dollars earned for every dollar invested. (Humes)

My age group all knew personally many WWII vets who benefitted directly from the GI Bill. My brother-in-law graduated from UB Medical School. Bob King and Hal Bergwall were Brown alums, others graduated from Princeton, and others Ivies as well as from Middlebury and Cornell. Benny Constantino was a UB grad, and the list could go on and on.

In the decades that followed, the GI Bill underwent changes. Korean War vets did not get a "full ride" but did receive a monthly check for $110 to cover tuition and living expenses.

My own experience with the GI Bill was proof of how transformative it could be for young men. I was the first member of my family to graduate from college, thanks to the bill.

Back to the early 50s, a few of us heard that the GI Bill would be ending. We needed money for education, so Zuke, Pete Warnock, Mac Sweeney, myself, and others agreed one afternoon at the Kenmore Tavern than we would ask to be drafted. We knew it would happen at some point, so why not now? We hiked downtown to the recruiting office – in the old Post office building in downtown Buffalo. A few weeks later we left Central Terminal and off we went to Fort Knox and thence overseas. A few years later we were back in college.

Mac Sweeney earned a degree from American University and a law degree from George Washington U., Pete Warnock graduated from UB and received a doctorate from Cornell. Myself, thanks to Uncle Sam, I finished at Canisius and used the GI Bill for a masters and doctoral work at Rutgers.

My own experience leads me to say: Thank You, Uncle Sam.

*Three GI's who made excellent use of the GI Bill. Left to right: Pete Warnock, Starr, M. Grant in South Korea*

# Honor Flights – For Vets
Originally printed October 2011

*For the past decade, the Honor Flight program has enabled thousands of vets (World War II) to fly to Washington for a visit to the magnificent monuments there. Enthusiastically received by the Greatest Generation, it has been very successful.*

I asked, "Do you remember Armistice Day in the 1940s?"

"Yeah," he exclaimed, "It was a day off of school and we also learned a new word—armistice."

As the Zuker put it, "That means guys stopped shooting each other." Essentially, "armistice" means calling a truce. World War I ended on November 11th, 1918. Shortly thereafter, President Wilson proclaimed Armistice Day a national holiday. In 1954, Armistice Day became Veterans Day, a day to honor veterans from all wars.

Over the years, veterans have been honored in various ways. Each November, they are remembered at national cemeteries. I have been fortunate to have visited Normandy; the Punchbowl overlooking Honolulu, Hawaii; Fort Rosecrans at Point Loma near San Diego; and Arlington National Cemetery. They are all magnificent sites. Boy Scouts, military units, American Legion posts and others gather to lay wreaths and place flags and participate in patriotic ceremonies honoring vets. There is a large veterans' section of Forest Lawn Cemetery.

In 2005, a new approach was initiated: The Honor Flight Program. The program brings World War II (WWII) vets from throughout the U.S. to Washington D.C. to visit the WWII Memorial which was completed in 2004. Since its inception, well over 100,000 vets have participated. The flight program really "took off."

Here is how it works from Buffalo. Vets apply to the local organization. A date is selected. Early on flight day, the vets assemble at Buffalo Niagara International Airport at 6AM. Each vet meets with a "guardian" who accompanies him or her the entire day. Paperwork is completed, and once aboard, breakfast is furnished.

Upon arrival in Washington, buses take vets and guardians to the WWII memorial on the National Mall. Lunch is served nearby. They also stop at the Vietnam and Korean War Memorials, after which they are bused to Arlington National Cemetery where they visit the awesome Iwo Jima Memorial. Dinner follows at a local restaurant and then the honored guests are bused back to the airport.

Upon return home, they are invariably met by hundreds of cheering supporters showing gratitude for the service the veterans performed for their country generations earlier.

The Honor Flight Program is conducted by non-profit organizations and is offered at no cost to veterans. Volunteers are the backbone of the program. A good example of a hardworking volunteer is Read Boeckel from Chicago. Boeckel is a former Marine who has participated in 55 flights. Typically, Read arises at 2AM, drives to the airport, completes paperwork, boards a flight as a guardian, serves as a bus captain, and then leads the Honor Guard ceremony at the WWII memorial.

The first flight from Buffalo took place on June 7th, 2008. Boeckel came from Chicago to accompany his father, Paul Boeckel, on this trip as his official guardian. Paul, a longtime Buffalo resident, served in the Army Air Corps in the Pacific Theater.

One high point for Paul and Read was finding themselves alongside retired Senator Robert Dole, a decorated vet. It was a great thrill for the Boeckels to converse with Sen. Dole, who has done so much for veterans for so long.

On the way to the airport, Read asked his dad if he wanted to call his wife of more than 65 years. He did, and said, "Bette, I just had the best day of my life."

Other Honor Flight participants share the enthusiasm of Boeckel. Joe Bittar, a Buffalonian, served in Germany immediately following WWII and then served again in Korea. He went on last May's Honor Flight. Bittar was ecstatic talking about the hundreds who were at the airport to greet him. The motorcycle escort that accompanied the buses from the airport to the Mall in D.C. had Joe feeling that he was either the Pope or the President.

Joe's friend, Clay Biehl, shares that same enthusiasm as he anticipates being on the next Honor Flight. Clay was inducted in 1943 and went to pilot training but before he finished, the demands for manpower after D-Day had Clay reassigned. He landed in Marseille, France and was promoted to First Sergeant in the 103rd Infantry Division. Then, it was full speed ahead. Clay's unit advanced through Southern France to battles in the Vosges Mountains, the Siegfried line, and finally the Battle of the Bulge. Following that, Clay and his fellow troopers entered Germany and a short time later liberated the Kaufering

Concentration Camp (a sub-camp of Dachau). Sgt. Biehl earned several medals and was discharged in 1946.

The Honors Flight Program has been a rousing success. It is a fitting tribute to the men and women who served in WWII.

*Clayt Biehl, Battle of Bulge, and Joe Bittar share Honor Flight stories*

# Chapter 10. Life in America – A Variety

*Seniors often think about the vast changes that have occurred in America in the last half century. New York City in the 50s, Florida as a temporary destination, a Catholic becoming President, and women reaching new heights were noteworthy topics. Also remembered happily were scouting days, and legendary figures.*

## 50 years ago - 1960 (The Last Hurrah!

Originally printed August 2010

*Remember some of the historic things that occurred a half a century ago: JFK, Cuba crisis, The St. Lawrence Seaway, a thrilling World Series, and the New Buffalo Bills.*

A presidential election year! Kennedy and Nixon monopolized the headlines. The television debates were watched by millions. Both candidates visited Buffalo's AUD (on separate nights) where 20,000 supporters cheered. Once the gravesites in Chicago were counted, Kennedy squeaked out a victory. Meanwhile the Civil Rights movement gained momentum. The students at the sit-ins in Greensboro North Carolina epitomized the heroics of the Southern non-violence campaign. Globally, the Cold War continued. The new Communist leader of Cuba, Fidel Castro, flirted with Russia while antagonizing the U.S. However Havana continued to play baseball against the Buffalo Bisons in the International League. Soviet Premier Nikita Khrushchev verbally attacked the United States and the UN over the U-2 incident.

188

Locally, despite a drop in population, the city of Buffalo seemed to be doing fairly well. The economy was booming; employment was healthy. Mammoth auto factories and chemical plants along the Niagara River and Buffalo River were humming and Big steel was never bigger. Bethlehem had a work force of 20,000, a veritable city itself. USW workers like "Lackawanna Mike" Langan garnered a heap of overtime while sweating before the Open Hearth. Some accounts had at least 50 saloons stretching along Route 5 across from the monstrous steel plant serving the needs of the hard hats. Check cashing was big business at Curley's Bar, Stosh's Saloon and Chester's Tavern. It was a free service provided you downed a boilermaker (usually a Simons Old Abbey or an Iroquois and a shot of Corbys).

On the other hand, some local officials and promoters counted on the St. Lawrence Seaway (recently completed) as being a boon for Buffalo. How wrong could they possibly be??, It was emphatically the opposite of a plus for the area.

The Sports Scene. The country was electrified by the World Series. It pitted the NY Yankees (as usual) against the Pittsburgh Pirates (rather unusual). The Yanks had the power and showed it by blasting the Bucs in three games; however the Pirates squeaked out three very close victories. So the 7th game – tied at 9-9 in the 9th set the stage for Bill Mazeroski's HR. One for the ages! They danced in the streets of Pittsburgh; the Rasmussens, O'Learys and Rooneys and the rest of the Steel City fans partied far beyond the Golden Triangle. Years later the section of the Forbes Field fence, over which the Mazeroski blast had traveled, still sits as a relic in the modern Pirate ballpark. Most Buffalo fans cheered for the Yankees, some were pleased with the Pirate miracle. Pittsburgh was closer to Buffalo and local big league fans occasionally boarded promoter Andy Moynihan's bus to travel there for a Sunday double header.

Earlier in the baseball season, Buffalo born Warren Spahn tossed a no-hitter for the Milwaukee Braves, his 20th victory of the year. In Denver Arnold Palmer shot a 65 in golf to win the U.S. Open. Many called it "the "greatest comeback ever."

The big sports news for the locals was the return of professional football. Ralph Wilson invested a small sum, the local media gave enthusiastic support, fan support could have been better, and the Bills went to work. The first season left something to be desired. But it was a beginning. Lou Saban and Jack Kemp and Elbert D. would build on those beginnings and bring championships to the city.

The local entertainment scene was going strong, an indication that the city still had some major city attributes. Downtown had not yet been abandoned at nightfall.

Johnny Pineapple and his orchestra played at the Statler; at the Dellwood Ballroom, the over 30 crowd could dance weekly to the music of Harold Austin with an occasional appearance by the great Ray Manuszewski. In the plush Town Casino top flight entertainers including the Ames Brothers and Paul Anka appeared. At the Glen Casino the summer bill featured Sammy Davis, Frankie Avalon, Andy Williams, and Connie Francis. The Castle on Eggert near Sheridan featured Al Hibbler, and also the Woody Herman band.

Crystal Beach featured Tommy Dorsey and Warren Covington and the Glenn Miller band under the direction of Ray McKinley. Melody Fair in North Tonawanda staged Broadway caliber plays including Pay Joey, South Pacific, Carousel and West Side Story.

And in Offermann Stadium in the summer of 1960 an absolutely superb jazz festival took place. Several legends or future ones played, including Dave Brubeck, Dizzy Gillespie, Gene Krupa, Louis Armstrong, Oscar Peterson, the Duke and the Count and Dinah Washington. Admission: $2 - $5. A real bargain! It had to be as good as the famous Newport Jazz festival that year, but the Buffalo one was held without the riots that accompanied the music extravaganza in Rhode Island.

Definitely worth noting too: Conductor Josef Krips led the Buffalo Philharmonic in celebrating its 25th anniversary, and Clayton Freiheit, highly recommended by the renowned Marlon Perkins, was appointed chief curator of the Buffalo Zoo.

Good things were happening in the Buffalo area in 1960!

*1960 First Presidential Debate, Kennedy - Nixon*

*Pirates beat Yankees in 1960 World Series. Perhaps the most famous series ever*

*The mammoth: Bethlehem Steel Plant. Lackawanna, NY 1960 - 20,000 employees*

# Crashing the Glass Ceiling
Originally printed December 2016

*Buffalo has had many outstanding women who have made major contributions to our area. Their numbers continue to increase.*

Donna Fernandes recently announced her retirement as the Director of the Buffalo Zoo; Sister Denise Roche, the seemingly ageless President of D'Youville College, retired a short time ago. Who's next: JoAnn Falletta?

We, in WNY, have been blessed with three super women of superior ability, managing cherished Buffalo institutions.

When Donna Fernandes arrived to take over the Buffalo Zoo, one of the oldest in the US, the institution was on its last legs. She worked wonders. I have been a zoo fan for many years, though I know Zilch about Zoology. Spending years attending sporting events and conferences across the country I have often took an extra day or two to visit a zoo or a national park. I suppose I could say that my fondness for zoos, like many of the After 50 readers, dates back to the days of Eddie the Monkey and Big Frank, the Elephant in the 1940s. But I have always felt that our zoo should be three times larger so it would be on par with the great Ohio zoos in Toledo, Columbus, and Cincinnati. Nevertheless Fernandes has done miracles with the zoo's 25 acres. Big is not necessarily best, as Zuke once said. Quality is what counts, and our Buffalo Zoo is top notch.

The same can be said for our Buffalo Philharmonic Orchestra in the hands of JoAnn Falletta. Maestro Falletta has brought world renowned talent to our magnificent Kleinhans Music Hall, and has proven to be one of the great conductors in our fair land. Thanks to her, our mid-size city has a prominent place in the nation's musical landscape.

Sister Denise Roche is in that triumvirate of trailblazing Buffalo Women. As the longtime president of D'Youville she has put that college on the map, making it a significant institution of higher learning in New York State. At the same time Roche and D'Youville have played a major role in the rejuvenation of Buffalo's West Side.

Upon retirement, having done so well in her position, Denise Roche is now heading up the Niagara Frontier Transportation Authority.

Check the Buffalo News and the internet for much more on the accomplishments of these three very accomplished women. They certainly crashed through some sort of glass ceilings. By the way, where did that phrase, "Glass Ceiling" originate? Checking Google, which is not always reliable, it notes that the phrase came about some twenty years ago with Big Business and Wall Street. Women were not able to break through the glass ceiling of the massive board rooms in Manhattan. That still is often the case.

Jump ahead to the election year of 2016. Hillary Clinton did not make it to the top position in the land; thus did not break through the ultimate glass ceiling. The result: many young women, many little girls were disappointed.

A segue - Instead of glass ceiling, more to my liking is the metaphor: "Is the glass half full or half empty?" I am a firm believer that the glass for women is half full and rising. With Hillary as a candidate for the Presidency, even more water is in that glass.

For us senior citizens, think about how far women have come. Think back to 1950. How many women held public office? Clare Booth Luce? She was our first major ambassador (Italy). Eleanor Roosevelt? She actually did not hold a public office but she surely ranks as one of the best known women ever.

Girls back in the 1950s, graduated high school then sought out marriage prospects or trained to be teachers or nurses. The glass ceiling was solid; the glass was quite empty.

Oh there was the occasional exception. Locally Mary Killeen became a lawyer, eventually a judge.

There were also exceptions on the national level. One of my favorites was Rachel Carlson, of "Silent Spring" fame. Babe Didrikson Zaharias was an outstanding all around Olympic athlete.

In the 60s the women, feminist, movement picked up steam.

Betty Friedan's best seller, "The Feminine Mystique" proved inspirational, maybe even revolutionary. Colleges throughout the country opened their doors to women. They entered in droves. Upon graduation women entered an ever expanding job market.

A personal note: When I became Director of Athletics, early 70s, no female in the entire US played an NCAA sport. Congress passed Title IX. Slowly at first (bureaucracy moves at a snail pace sometimes) girls began to participate. Initially enforcement dragged, but by the 1990s the floodgates opened.

In government, it was a somewhat similar development. Women politicians were elected to congress, the senate, and to state legislatures. Many became governors. We now have three women Supreme Court justices.

There still is some distance to go to fill up that glass. There needs to be more progress for women in the boardrooms as well as in the public office arena. But in the not too distant future, I believe we will see a woman in the highest office in the land. Madame President will be right up there with the likes of Margaret Thatcher and Angela Merkel.

(*Satcher*)

## Charles Yeager - Sixty years ago a Celebrity
Originally printed November 2012

*Charles Yeager of a prominent Buffalo family served as manager for the Yale Football Team. In the last game of the 1952 season against archrival Harvard, the Yale coach put Yeager in at the end of the game. Yeager caught a pass for the point after touchdown, and is forever immortalized as a legend of the college gridiron.*

60 years ago Charlie Yeager became an instant celebrity. And who you may ask is Charlie Yeager?? Charlie is a well-known Buffalonian, a veritable bon vivant, and sportsman as well. He was a tennis partner of Ralph Wilson of the Bills for decades. Charlie continues to play – in his 80s - at the Buffalo Tennis and Squash Club. He was also adept at both squash and handball. He still plays golf. Recently he recorded a hole in one at Cherry Hill. He has always been somehow involved in football. He loves the sport; attends the Bills' quarterback club luncheons regularly and has for many decades. He grew up in Kenmore, graduated from Nichols and Yale and became a successful insurance man in Buffalo.

So – how did he become an INSTANT CELEBRITY?

Here is how it happened. In his senior year, Charlie was the manager of the Yale football team. It was the 1952 season and Yale had a very good team. At practices, Chuck would often catch passes from assistant coach Angelo Bertelli. Yes, the Heisman trophy winner from Notre Dame who was an assistant coach at Yale. Head Coach Jordan Olivar noticed Yeager's enthusiasm for football; he said he would give him a chance for the extra point if the opportunity arose.

That opportunity came in THE GAME, as the annual Harvard-Yale clash was called. Things developed perfectly. The plans had called for Charlie to suit up at halftime. Covertly he did that, donning jersey 99, the only one that fit his 5' 5", 138 lb. frame. He sat quietly at the end of the bench and waited. Near the end of the 3rd quarter, QB Ed Molloy completed his 4th TD pass to put Yale ahead 40-7. Now for the point after.

Immortality beckoned. The coach sent Yeager in; he lined up at right end. The ball was snapped to QB Molloy – he ran to his right. Yeager was temporarily blocked by a Harvard defensive man, shoved into his own tackle, righted himself then sped into the end zone. Molloy spotted him and lobbed a pass. Yeager caught it and hurried right on through the end zone out of danger of any Harvard player taking a shot at him.

A legend was born. Immortality achieved. Yeager's photo adorned the fence outside of Mory's, of "Tables Down at Mory's" fame. Photos on that fence were usually reserved for Yale captains. The story made Life, Time, Sat. Evening Post, and the New York Times. An Associated Press poll called it the most humorous incident of the 1952 season.

Even the legendary Red Smith weighed in. He wrote that Harvard suffered additional humiliation when the 41st point was scored by "an undergraduate custodian of used towels." Charlie chuckles at that line written by, perhaps, the greatest sports writer ever.

Initially Harvard's reaction was mixed. Some thought it was a shabby gimmick. Most came around to accept it for what it was, and in the years that followed Yeager was embraced by Harvard men. Some years ago the Harvard club of Syracuse presented Yeager with a Harvard Chair, which, to this day, he still uses. Yeager's long time business partner, Webb Durant, was a Harvard grad. In fact, Webb was present at THE GAME.

Over the years the celebrity ride continued. On the 50th anniversary, both the Boston Globe and New York Times did stories, as did many other media outlets. The Times article, "A Point in Harvard's Side" was written by another accomplished sports writer, George Sullivan. He noted that any hard feelings had vanished. The Times' story concludes that on that day the Yale Manager "made his point at Harvard Stadium and instantly became a legend at two great universities."

In fact Charlie Yeager entered the college football record book as the highest scoring team manager in the United States and this was long before Notre Dame's Rudy made headlines in the 1993 movie.

# Florida – a great place to visit – But!
Originally printed April 2012

*For decades, Buffalonians have joined the thousands migrating to Florida to escape the Northern winters. Students on winter break flocked to Ft. Lauderdale, the well-heeled flocked to Palm Beach and Miami, and later to the Gulf Coast. But for many snowbirds, it was nice to return to the old hometown.*

The 1960 film, "Where the Boys Are?" summons up fond memories for the "after 50 crowd." I remember it like yesterday, standing outside the Elbow Room watching guys and gals passing by - they were always passing by – some awestruck at the presence of Golden Boy, Paul Hornung, the All American halfback from Notre Dame. He too was on Spring break.

As for myself, I had returned to college after a stint in Korea, and was ready to join the mass migration south. My GI Bill did not cover trips to Florida so I did what many others did; found a ride in a banged up Chevy, chipped in for the gas money, and crashed in a motel "suite" with a number of other guys (whom I rarely saw), and spent my disposable cash on food and drink (mostly the latter).

It was a harrowing trip, over winding country roads through Virginia and the Carolinas, no interstate yet. But it was worth it: beer, broads, and beaches waited in South Florida. The Ft. Lauderdale area grew like wildfire after WWII and in the 50s it was a virtual metropolis. Luxurious hotels lined the strip; the moneyed set purchased high-rise condos along the Galt mile and Joe DiMaggio and the Yankees were in spring training nearby. Guys and gals covered the beach and packed the bars. What a place! I mean is this Shangri La or what?

Florida was far different than today. Northerners got their first glimpse of segregation as they discovered the little signs saying "Whites only" and "Colored" affixed to water fountains and restroom doors. There was little concern for urban sprawl or tawdry development. The Everglades were still pristine; panthers were not yet near extinction. As one drove over Alligator Alley to the west coast and then north – still not much development was seen until you arrived near the old folks encampments in the St. Pete's area. Other than the baseball spring training sites spread throughout various parts of the state, and Ester Williams performing at the Cypress Gardens, not much else was going on. The grapefruit league was a bonus because real fans got a chance to sit in a folding chair near the outfield – for free.

Florida has changed over the past half century. The authorities grew tired of the unruly mobs in Lauderdale; the students obliged and migrated north to Daytona, and later west along the Gulf Coast. By the end of the century, affluent students were spending holidays in the Caribbean, Mexico and beyond. Still many continued to come to Florida – all ages and shapes. Many stayed.

The retired, including many on public pension, had money to burn. Some purchased a condo, a second residence, in the Sunshine State. Disney World opened in the 70s, Orlando mushroomed, and the Interstate 4 corridor took off; so did Cape Kennedy and the Gulf Coast. The Villages became a veritable metropolis almost overnight; a mega community where golf carts seemed to be most everywhere and walkers and wheelchairs were everywhere else. The state's population soared.

Despite the best efforts of preservationists and the likes of Miami Herald's prize winning author, Carl Hiassen, the crowds kept coming. Hiassen's somewhat comical mysteries, highly critical of developers, politicians, and the wealthy tourists of the North, are great reads. Incidentally, one vacationer did spot a lone orange grove on the outskirts of Citrus County and a few venturesome types found areas of solitude in the vicinity of Cedar Key. But for the most part the land of the alligators and orange groves has given way to Burmese pythons and senior communities.

The sun is the magnet. It's "gotta" be. It draws tourists and new residents, those with golf clubs and swimsuits and those bearing gifts: Sahlen's Hot Dogs, Weber's mustard, Kummelweck rolls, and sponge candy (Do people still eat that?).

The winner in this Florida quagmire (at least it sometimes seems like that) is the occasional tourist. He "has it made" in that there is always someone to visit, a relative, old friend, new acquaintance, or former co-worker. It might be Aunt Pat in Gainesville, Chet, a "5 handicapper" in Naples, Tim Wilcox, bar entrepreneur near South Beach, volunteer fireman Ted in Crystal River, or even the famous Doyles of Pompano Beach. Having worn out the welcome mats, the peripatetic visitor can head back up North. Other transplanted Northerners might join him, agreeing with Donn Esmonde that Buffalo is a pretty nice place to live. Stereotypes notwithstanding, the weather is good - there is a notable absence of natural disasters. True, the city is not the great metropolis it once was, the downtown is often dreary (Tom Brady had a point) but again, to paraphrase Esmonde, we should recognize that we are a mid-sized city, but one with wonderful amenities. You've heard it all before; a magnificent Philharmonic, art galleries, plenty of live theater, beaches, ski slopes, parks, and architectural gems. Located just 90 miles to the North is a world class city. Of course, we also have a natural wonder, known locally simply as "The Falls", in our backyard.

Yes, Florida is great - once in a while.

## Happy Birthday - Boy Scouts
Originally printed June 2010

*60 – 70 years ago, Boy Scouts was a major activity. Weekend camping and weeks at summer camp at Camp Ti-Wa-Ya-Ee were terrific experiences and are the "stuff" of lasting memories.*

Happy 100 years old. The Boy Scouts have been a positive force in American life for a century. Sean Beiter, local head of the Scouts, recently wrote eloquently of the scouting values that benefit our society, noting that the experience teaches valuable lessons while instilling lasting values: God, country, family, and respect for leaders. And who can forget the oath: A Scout is trustworthy, loyal, helpful . . . etc. I remember that as well as my army serial number, pounded into my fearful head by a screaming brute of a sergeant.

I am proud to have been a scout, however briefly. That was over a half century ago. Presently, my son in law and my two grandsons are involved. In fact, after being away from scouting for 60 years, Paul Reister, local scout chieftain, talked me into becoming a kind of adjunct scoutmaster. My grandsons are just as much into little league type sports, as any other red-blooded American kid. Fortunately, they make time for scouting. The scouts serve nicely as an antidote for too much obsession with sports.

The past decades have witnessed a big decline in Boy Scout numbers. Many other activities compete for kids' time: video games, WiFi, and sports of every sort. Nothing wrong with all that, but the old rule of everything in moderation would be wise to follow. It seems absurd for a young high school football player to spend 9 months of the off-season, pumping weight, trying to perfect his pass rush. Do those budding behemoths need more common sense?

In addition to the great values that Scouting teaches, and the sense of pride and achievement that comes with earning a merit badge, the fact is that the scouting experience is just plain fun, especially the camping part. I still reminisce about overnights in the lean-tos at the Loggers campsite when I get together with Fring, Shoes, and Smitty, even after some 60 years. We foraged for logs for the campfires: I swear we thought of ourselves as George Washington's men at Valley Forge, saving civilization for our love ones.

For dinner - A can of Chef Boyardee spaghetti, opened with the best little can opener the world has ever known, from a World War II K-ration kit. Heat it in a mess kit pot over a struggling fire. Not exactly dining at the Ritz but who cared. We had a varied menu; Campbell beans, # 10 can, and some cookies (preferably toll house from Mom's oven) that would be shared with the local field mice as they crept under our bunks during the night. We had other good stuff from the war surplus stores on Main Street such as trenching tools and canteens with dents (we were sure these had survived Guadalcanal).

Later around a campfire, wrapped in an army surplus olive drab blanket, we swapped stories about our leaders, ex GIs, who were, at that time, down the road at the Holland Willows knocking down a few Genesee beers. When our leaders returned we listened to endless war stories: Iwo Jima, Guadalcanal, Bastogne, and more.

Summer camp was a completely different experience; more regulations, more varied activities but also lots of fun. Troop competitions, including sporting contests, campfire singing sessions as well as drinking lots of bug juice in the Long House mess hall were all part of the experience. So was standing at attention for the flag lowering ceremony. Arts and crafts were woven into the daily activities. We never seemed to grab on to those very much. But we did learn valuable, lifelong lessons about water safety, the buddy system, canoeing, and swimming.

A highlight for me was induction into the Order of the Arrow. All the scout troops assembled on Long House Hill. Those to be inducted stepped three paces in front of the ranks. Scout leaders, dressed as Indians and wearing grotesque masks, walked slowly with drums (tom-toms) beating and came to a halt in front of me. The "Chief" tapped me, while mumbling some Indian words. It was a solemn affair, but there was Shoes right behind me trying to make me laugh at the masked tappers. That evening the new inductees had to saw logs for firewood (one of the toughest jobs ever) and prepare council fires. Then we were led, blindfolded, along "secret" trails to observe Indian ritual and lore. Finally, we were taken to an isolated spot to spend the night alone under the stars. Wow. I figured I was a veritable Daniel Boone when it was all over.

More prosaic were the bi weekly patrol meetings at various members' homes. Attention was usually on refreshments. The favorite was Mr. Murphy's famous chocolate cake. Time was spent working on merit badges, tying a variety of knots, and doing camp preparation.

Then there was the annual Memorial Day Parade. It consisted of fleets of fire trucks, the local high school band and thousands of scouts in various stages of uniform dress. The kids from wealthy parents had the full shot (official cap, shirt, socks and pants that matched, etc.); others had the bare minimum, a scout shirt and kerchief and baggy everyday pants - Knickers, partly torn. Scouting was and is a truly wonderful experience. If our youth miss it, it's a big loss, and an even bigger loss for society.

*Eagle Scout presentation. Left to right: Commissioner Reister, Scout Master Joe Hassett, New Eagles Joey Hassett and Alex Harvey, and Scoutmaster Eric Harvey*

# The Big Apple – aka New York City, Circa. 1950

Originally printed November 2016

*The Carnegie Deli is closing! Yes, the famous landmark Deli around the corner from Carnegie Hall is no longer going to be serving huge corned beef on rye to visitors and regulars – as it has been doing since 1937.*

So I began reflecting. NYC! How has it changed? Many of my peers first encountered NYC in the decade after World War II, myself included. Tom Comer and I decided we would head to "The Big Apple" (that is what we hip teenagers called it) to see our buddy, Joe, who had recently moved there. We boarded a Greyhound bus for an uncomfortable 10 hour trip, no interstates then, which brightened only when the fabulous New York skyline appeared on the early morning horizon as the bus sped through New Jersey toward Manhattan.

The bus dropped us off at the 63rd YMCA, now near the site of Lincoln Center. The Y was the place for kids to stay, low budget. Another pal, Dave Costello, the Elmira kid, stayed, about the same time, at the Sloan House, an even larger Y, located on 34th street. Our Y director, showed us to our stark bare bones room and then asked if we knew anything about homosexuals, of course, being streetwise 16 year olds from Kenmore, we quickly said "Yea." He told us to be cautious.

Our trip was outstanding, 65 years later many memories are still vivid. We took tours around the city. Hey, that is what any first time visitor would do. One was the Circle Line cruise, a half-day trip that circled the island of Manhattan. Next was a bus trip that went throughout Manhattan, from Battery Park then North to Harlem and covering many of the famous points in between. I recall the Fulton Fish Market (Al Smith grew up there), Wall Street, Herald Square (Macys and Gimbels), Union Square where various screwballs, including a variety of Marxists, could shout and carry on. We drove through the Bowery, (my bet is that millennials have never even heard of the infamous place), then past Chinatown, Greenwich Village, along 5th Avenue past St. Patrick's Cathedral, Radio City, through Central Park and back to Times Square.

Times Square – for many of us Times Square is New York. But it has changed mightily. Back then: Newsstands on virtually every corner offering Hollywood movie magazines, e.g. silver screen, and stacks of newspapers (NYC had 7 dailies then). Tom and I got a big thrill when Gus, a quintessential New York, who ran one of the newsstands, asked us to watch it for him briefly (while he left to place a bet). We did and so we could boast that we sold newspapers in Times Square - I think we actually sold one?

We checked out the Hotel Astor, (the signature hotel in the Square) to look around. You could walk into the Lobby, look around, walk out again on to Broadway, no metal detectors, cameras, or armies of security guards (free and open - what a different time!). At the south end of Times Square stood the iconic Times Building; at its base was a newsstand selling newspapers from all over the world. Next to it was an MP station, where the slickly dressed military gendarmes were on the lookout for AWOL troopers from Fort Dix.

Around the corner on 42nd street were numerous movie theaters (porn had not yet taken over). Further up Broadway, in the 40s and 50s, were the even more numerous Broadway theaters.

Times Square has always been marked by many big billboards; two stand out in my memory. One featured a Hollywood celeb blowing smoke rings (for Camel Cigarettes) out into Times Square; the other was for Bond Clothes (every suit with two pair of pants) which was highlighted with waterfalls as part of the billboard.

Jack Dempsey's Broadway bar, along with Sardi's restaurant, which famously catered to glamorous show people, was nearby. So was the Latin Quarter with a bevy of beauties constantly parading by on the stage. We settled for the Horn and Hardart automat. Put your nickels in the slot and receive a sandwich! The automat was vintage New York. I sat down with my lunch, and out of nowhere another guy, a complete stranger sits down next to me, eats his sandwich and leaves without saying a word. I was puzzled, but quickly determined that this is New York City. And the coming and going of anonymous people happens regularly.

Baseball was really big then, and especially in NYC. We took a bus, only white guys on it, up through Harlem to the Polo grounds. No problem back then. We also stopped by Birdland. We felt compelled to, since Zuke and Shoes were heavily into the Jazz scene.

A few other tourist sites were mandatory. These included The Port Authority Bus terminal with its sea of humanity at commuter times and the iconic Grand Central and Penn Stations. Also on that route was Madison Square Garden located close to the Port Authority. No World Trade Center then; the three tallest buildings were the Empire State, the Chrysler, and Radio City. We viewed the great metropolis from the top of Radio City. Breathtaking!

By the way, we did visit our pal, Joe. In fact he could drive so he took us to Jones Beach (to ogle the young beauties), and to Coney Island for a Nathan's hot dog and a ride on the Parachute Jump.

We had a busy week. But In New York there is always more. It was and is the greatest city in the world. I could hardly wait to return, which I would many times. More later!

*WWII Aircraft Carrier Saratoga leaves NY Harbor*

The Buffalo Braves (Basket Ball)
Bob Meadows